THE PORTRAIT

P.R. BROWN

THE PORTRAIT

P.R. BROWN

DB
PUBLISHING

By the same author

Non-fiction:

The Gods of Our Time
Dreams and Illusions Revisited
The Mountain Dwellers
Language and Life

Fiction:

The Mirror Men
The Treadmillers
The Shadow People
Circle Walker
Diary of the Last Man
The Spare Room, Of Elves and Men
Undeliverable Letters, Unreachable Galaxies, or The Man in the Old Bowler Hat

First published 2025 by DB Publishing, an imprint of JMD Media Ltd, Nottingham, United Kingdom.

ISBN 9781780916675

Printed in the UK

To my cousin Judith, who remembers my father with much affection.

THE PORTRAIT

I thought you left me crying all alone in a troubled land,
But then I heard you calling
And felt the warmth of your outstretched hand.
I know they say you have passed away, no longer here to guide,
But I hear your voice on the summer breeze
And see you face in the clouds where you abide
(Song for the Uncommon Common Man)

Despite his many and varied material achievements, his burgeoning technology, his resilience and ability to adapt, man's much-vaunted civilisation, his humanity, what the religious might call his 'soul', hangs by a slender thread. Were it not for the 'uncommon common man', that thread would snap asunder, and it might well do so notwithstanding. Meanwhile, the wise and the worried hope to live out their lives under the tender gaze of a loving God, knowing full well that love is a sure gateway to sorrow.

P.R. Brown

CONTENTS

The portrait of my father, Percival Richard Daniel Brown

1

HAUNTED

Even then, at the tender age of eight or nine, I wondered how they managed to build houses like that – long strips of houses called 'terraced' on the steep slopes of grassy hills, with their backs perched precariously on the brow of dangerous descents. But that's how it was in the valleys of the Land of My Fathers, there where the 'rape of the fair country' was brazenly, unapologetically, committed in broad daylight – which brings me to aunt Lewi (pronounced Loowee, with stress on the first syllable).

Aunt Lewi's house was an end of terrace house and, no doubt like all the others in that row, had a dark interior, the light struggling to breach the small and none-too-clear windows that were the norm in those days and in houses like that. The skimpy kitchen, where food was prepared on a black-leaded oven, was particularly devoid of light and was located at the rear of the house so that the windows, such as they were, looked out and down the grassy hills. Grey, cold, concrete steps in disconcertingly steep decline led down, down, down to a feeble pretence of a 'back garden' which was in fact no more than a threadbare patch of grass, long neglected, and defiled here and there with domestic rubbish long discarded, like old saucepans devoid of their handles, the skeleton of an old, rusted pushchair and suchlike – altogether no sight for sore eyes. Back gardens were normally used on washing days when clothes were hung on lines to dry. But this patch of rubbished grass hadn't seen a washing line in many years, because only the young and the brave and the fit could possibly attempt that perilous descent down those wretched

9

stone steps in the expectation of reaching the bottom in one piece. Aunt Lewi was no longer young, and certainly no longer fit.

Aunt Lewi was not *my* aunt. She was my maternal grandmother's sister and therefore properly the real aunt of my mother and my aunt Betty, my grandmother's daughters. Aunt Betty, a heavily built lady then in her late 30s, would sometimes take me with her when asked by my grandmother to help aunt Lewi to do her housework. I say 'help', but really poor aunt Lewi was incapable of lifting a finger to help herself in this matter, being obese and crippled with rheumatoid arthritis. Harold, her husband, was a retired coal miner and suffered from emphysema as a reward for years of burrowing underground like some hapless escapee in some dark fantasy contrived to frighten children, and adults with little imagination. Harold did escape, but only at the cost of any real quality of life. He was constantly short of breath and wheezed every time he spoke.

As for aunt Lewi's house itself, there is really little more to say, apart from noting the damp odour that pervaded it throughout – not forgetting the enormous amount of dusty clutter that resisted the attempts of poor aunt Betty to give sideboards and other flat, wooden surfaces a thorough polishing. But she did the best she could, while I stood around and about or followed her from room to room like a junior foreman, watching her flick dusters. I remember being assailed by the strong aroma of wax polish and the odour of mustiness, the one in combat with the other like two ethereal gladiators. There were no aerosol sprays then and no polish to be shot through the air in a cloud of particles from a tin. Waxy polish came in tins and was transferred to dusters and then applied to wooden furniture in a frenzy. One duster to polish, and one to shine – all very hard work, not at all for young hands. I followed aunt Betty around, astonished at her masculine energy and her determination to leave everything in a far better state than she had found it. She worked very hard, but always in good humour, sometimes pretending to polish my nose or dust down my pullover.

Now as I recall, my visits to aunt Lewi's house were never made on dry, sunny days. It was as though the sun had decided to give such houses in such streets in such small Welsh villages as these a very wide berth. The sun and the rain were in collusion, for it often drizzled under forlorn skies, so that the grey weather seemed to mirror the depressingly dark interior of the house. This I suppose is one reason why I never descended those stone steps all the way down to that postage stamp of a garden below – that, and the fact that I had been told not to attempt the perilous journey. So the garden at the rear of the house was out of

10

bounds. I let it be, though interestingly enough it has never had the decency to follow suit, but has somehow made a lasting impression and even now refuses to dissolve into the irrecoverable ether of memory.

I ask myself why I should bother to recount these visits to aunt Lewi's house. She and her husband Harold were kindly people, but it's not as though I was ever spoiled with affection, not even once. I was never offered ice-cream or sweet cakes. I was never bounced on Harold's knees near the fireplace and told stories of fantastic creatures of bygone days. He might have told me what it was like to navigate your way in darkness through deep underground tracks, but he never did. Of course, the poor fellow was too busy coping with his ailments and no doubt regretting his inability to do more than he could about the house. He seemed to spend most of those grey days sitting by the hearth, staring at the small glow in the grate and gingerly putting a few more coals on the fire just to keep it going with the minimum of expense. Wherever I was in that house I seemed to hear occasional coughs produced in an aura of breathlessness.

After a while, these visits ceased, and then I remember hearing of Harold's demise. Aunt Lewi was soon to follow. When she died, my grandmother was the only surviving child in a family of 16 siblings. How their parents had managed to bring them all up in circumstances of material hardship astonishes and puzzles me – it also earns them the greatest respect. Yes, but hardship and large families were considered natural in those days and in such communities largely went unquestioned. That was how it was in the Land of my Fathers where – at least to most minds – the rich were unmistakably rich, the poor unmistakably poor, and there was nothing much in-between.

I ask myself again why I bother to recall those visits to aunt Lewi's house. But, of course, the question is quite wrong. It's not a matter of 'bothering', for that would imply that I have some choice, whereas I have no choice at all. The truth is, those visits *haunt* me, and, as far as I know, we do not *choose* to be haunted. In fact, the more you try to get away from such ghosts, the more they are attracted to you. The more you try to lose them, the more they follow you, like a stray dog. Now this may begin to sound odd or somewhat eccentric to some, but it seems to me that not all haunting, not all ghosts, are sinister and therefore unwelcome. On the contrary, if I say, as I most certainly do say, that I am haunted by the memory of my visits to aunt Lewi, I must also say here and now that I am haunted in the manner of a kindly ghost, not one that is hell-bent on causing me the discomfort and pain of fear. Her house might well have been imagined as the scene of some unspeakable evil – but it did not and does not present itself like this to me. It was no version of '10 Rillington Place'!

It is a well-documented fact, with no less than medical testimony to support it, that long-term memory improves with age. It should come as no surprise therefore that my memory of those visits to aunt Lewi is clearer now than ever it was. It comes as no surprise that I can relive those visits as though they were yesterday, smell the odours as though they were in the air right now, and even seem to stand at the top of those dreadful stone steps and peer down, down, down into that sad excuse for a garden below. (One might even speculate, of course with tongue abundantly in cheek, whether, should one live long enough, past experiences could actually become *real* again! But I am not at all sure that such an event would be entirely welcome. Better to settle for clarity over reality, I should say.)

I think what I am driving at is that being haunted is not necessarily either a bad or an unpleasant thing. Perhaps we can learn a great deal from a haunting, from the ghosts that haunt us – perhaps we can learn things which may still be of service to us or even improve our lives. And perhaps it is similar to dreams, for we can learn a great deal from them if we take the trouble to try to understand them. I am taking the liberty of repeating the word 'perhaps', because in such foggy matters as these one should never claim to be the repository of all knowledge or the fount of all wisdom. A little uncertainty is a humbling, not to say humanising, thing.

Let me put the matter like this: I am not forgetting how frightening and unsettling the experience or feeling of being haunted may be, any more than I question the great discomfort nightmares can and frequently do engender, but, in the pages that follow, my focus is elsewhere – on the sunny uplands, not on the dark valleys below.

Having said that, I must confess to a certain ambivalence. While it is true that the memory of visits to aunt Lewi do not fill me with discomfort, let alone horror, I feel a general distaste for strange places, I mean places which are unfamiliar to me, especially grey, neglected places. I am not even sure that 'distaste' is quite the right word – perhaps it is a kind of distaste mingled with fascination. Or perhaps I find such places magical, but I cannot decide whether the magic is sinister or amicable. However I try to describe it, the effect on me of unfamiliar places, streets, hills, houses is undeniable and undeniably profound. When, where and how these feelings began I cannot say. No doubt they had very early beginnings. At an early age, in the first decade after the second world war, I would accompany aunt Betty to a large covered market where second-hand clothes and fabrics were sold. The stuff was not neatly laid out at ground level but presented in bundles ranged on long wooden tiers that seemed to young eyes to reach to the roof, so that you had to walk up and down, and along each tier, to inspect what was on offer – yes, an odd arrangement. This and the odour of old clothes must have filled me with the kind of feeling I have tried unsuccessfully to describe. The size of the hall and the large numbers of shoppers it attracted might well have unsettled me with the possibility of getting lost. Carried away by the wonder of it all, and whenever aunt Betty let go my small hand to feel the quality of fabrics, I must have felt on the edge of my little world and in danger of falling off into an abyss. I never ran about to explore, or play hide and seek with my aunt. I had no curiosity. I was overawed by the oddness of it all, the odour of a multitude of old fabrics (neither pleasant nor unpleasant), the hustle and bustle, the faint echo in the huge vault of a roof. It was unfamiliar and faintly disconcerting.

No doubt the line between fascination and discomfort is often hard to draw, as is that between discomfort and pain. Aunt Lewi's house was also disconcerting – but neither painful nor intimidating. Hauntings which are very far from intimidating are those that fascinate me more than those that are.

We know that being haunted may be painful, like a bad memory that forces itself upon you, triggered in some way, or totally un-triggered as though having its own momentum and invading your space when you least expect it and are least prepared for it.

Yet there are hauntings peopled by ghosts of quite another character, ghosts that provide guidance, companionship and a most soothing balm in a world that seems far from welcoming and itself full of demons – which brings me to a very special portrait and its most remarkable effects, a matter on which I can claim to speak with some unique authority.

2

UNREMARKABLE BEGINNINGS

It is, or ought to be, a well-attested fact that the most remarkable phenomena may have the most unremarkable beginnings. What, for example, could be less remarkable than the decision to hang the portrait of a deceased loved one on the wall?

The portrait in question is of my late father. I say 'late', but I should say very late since he had been deceased for several decades before it was decided to make an enlargement from a small photograph and hang the portrait on the wall on the landing between two bedrooms and close to the privy. The portrait was a sepia photograph taken when my father must have been in his early to mid-20s. The face is of an intelligent young man with a smile as enigmatic as that of the Mona Lisa's. His eyes I remember were a penetrating blue though this cannot be properly guessed from the photograph. His aspect is fresh-looking, pleasant, tolerant and hopeful and as yet unblemished by the twin evils of time and men. The portrait suggests a calmness of mind and demeanour, and a simplicity that I myself have long ceased to possess or to expect from others. Young, healthy, hopeful, expectant of some good fortune along life's winding paths – you might almost hear him thinking that God's in his Heaven and all's right with the world.

The time would come when God would experience considerable discomfort, but I must hold the reins on this narrative and proceed slowly.

It was, as I say, quite unremarkable that a portrait of my father should be placed on the wall. Consequently, it was never remarked upon. All those entering and leaving their bedrooms would hardly notice it at all, while those hell-bent on reaching and leaving the privy would hardly be expected to give it a second glance. So there it stayed, proper and respected, but insignificant in the day-to-day run of things. Who would have thought that this head-and-shoulders photograph could hold such power and inspiration, housed in its plain and simple wooden frame? Come to think of it, in the world of art, a world about which I profess to know next to nothing, there must surely be some if not many instances in which the value or beauty of the frame far exceeds that of the painting within it.

I might mention here that the portrait was placed above a small writing bureau, at first quite coincidentally, though in fact most appropriately. The bureau was a Christmas present to me, at the unsuitable age of about nine, that my father had apparently insisted on buying. His argument, which was explained to me in subsequent years, was that it was an educational investment for later years of study. The fact remained that it was too big at the time it was given to me and too small when the time came for serious study. I have always consoled myself with the sentiment that it was the thought that counts. The fact that the bureau came from my father with the very best of intentions has endeared it to me all these years. Its sentimental value is naturally inestimable. And though it sits comfortably under the portrait of the donor in a permanent state of disuse as a place of study, it functions as a storage unit for the endless pieces of paper in the form of bills and notifications that are the poor stuff and substance of human civilisation. On this account alone, its location is assured – not downstairs amid the traffic of daily life, but out of sight and mind until the stairs, which my father called 'the wooden hill' as he piggy-backed me to bed, was attempted in a state of somnolence.

Sentimentality apart, there is a far deeper reason for calling attention to the writing bureau. Upon it is a burn mark from a lighted cigarette which must have rolled off an ashtray. The mark goes way down under the grain of the wood and makes an unmistakeable and indelible impression on the highly polished surface. Each time I see it I am reminded of my father's death, for the mark was made that very night. Someone must have lit a cigarette while my father was slumped in a chair, his having suffered what was then called a 'coronary thrombosis'. I had been sitting with him alone watching television, as was the routine every Saturday night, when he took a turn for the worse. I ran to my maternal grandmother's which was very close by and pretty soon the living room was occupied by three or four people apart from myself. I was 13, and my worst fears were realised that night, when my father's moans and groans of pain in the middle of many nights suddenly began to make some horrible sense. He had been looking grey, and the lines on his face seemed deeper than ever and his blue eyes less alert. I remember very clearly feeling afraid for him for ages before this night – afraid for myself, too, for I felt so close to my father that life without him seemed an intolerable prospect – which it turned out to be.

My grandmother left the room and came back a few minutes later with a small glass of brandy and water, while my father, still with us, looked ashen grey and seemed quite incapable of speech. I just stood there, watching, dumbstruck, and probably praying for a miracle. My grandmother put the glass of brandy and water to his lips. 'Here, drink this, my boy.' To this day, I cannot claim to know the rationale behind the glass of brandy. Did she think it might have revived him? Or did she believe that the spirits would deliver a fatal cardiac shock and put my father out of his misery in the absence of any hope of recovery? She seemed to act instinctively, as though she knew exactly what she was doing – for she was an old lady who had seen the face of death more than once. In any case, my father convulsed seconds later, and was no more.

My last image of my father was burned into my young psyche deeper than the burn in the wood of the writing bureau – his body limp and still in that armchair, a trickle of blood from the right-hand corner of his mouth. Then I was ushered quickly out of the room. It was dark outside, with, it seemed the stillness of death in the cold night air. I remember looking up into the night sky, as though appealing to some higher authority for an explanation. None came.

Then came several weeks, perhaps months, off school – a period in which I remember being addicted to aspirin, feeling perhaps that a daily dose would function to some degree as a palliative – or was I simply scared of following my father into the long goodnight of the poet? My eventual return to school was marked by a sympathetic audience with the headmaster, who expressed his condolences and said that the lack of tears was a sign of resilience of which my father would have been proud. And with that I returned to class and the long almost invariably uninspiring grind that is commonly called education. I say uninspiring, because learning cannot be inspiring unless teachers are inspired. The world is full of colour, yet the majority of teachers tended to teach only in black and white, and I daresay they still do.

That last impression of my father in death has haunted me all through my life – an exceptionally good man gone long before his time. And now I use the word 'haunted' advisedly, for it is the very purpose of this narrative to explain the nature of this haunting, how it has shaped my life, how it is a pain which, to quote Socrates, who was referring to something else, I would not exchange for any pleasure. For my father became a role model from the very start, from at least the very moment he departed this life. My memories of him have shaped my attitude to everyday events and made them a little more bearable than they would otherwise have been. They point to the importance of role models, the right kind of role models, in our lives. But I must make these memories speak for themselves, one by one in the narratives that follow. I feel I must do this in honour of my father, whose life was cut short at the age of 47, despite his participation in the war against Nazism, despite his being shot and wounded by the Vichy French, despite his meekness and mildness, despite his capacity for becoming far more than he was, despite his being an exceptionally good man, but then I must remind myself that those whom the gods love die young – but are we to thank the gods for this? We must trust that they know more than we do.

3

THERE ARE THOSE THAT READ, AND THOSE THAT READ

People say things like 'There are actors, and there are actors', or 'There are doctors, and there are doctors', or 'There are artists, and there are artists'. They mean that not all actors, or all doctors, or all artists are good at what they do. Some are better than others, some less conscientious than others.

If I say 'There are those that read, and those that read', I suppose I am pointing out that people read for different purposes and that purposes differ from one another. Reading a train timetable is not the same as reading for pleasure, and the latter is not the same as reading for philosophical enlightenment.

My father was a reader, and although he was fond of history, the only book I ever found him reading was the Bible. It became a family joke, unbeknown to him, that he would read the Bible even if the house were on fire. 'Tell your father the dinner's ready,' my mother would reprovingly say. 'You know where he is.' Yes, I did know where he was – invariably in the garden shed, bespectacled and engrossed in what I later realised was some part of the New Testament. He kept his Bible in a green plastic bag in a drawer in the sideboard, and whenever you failed to find it there, you knew where he was and what he was doing. He kept the shed tidy and could find any tool at a moment's notice. He was a handyman and could turn his hand to most things, making something out of wood and a few nails. But the shed was also his retreat.

After his passing, I remember looking at the flyleaf of his copy of the Bible and finding there, written in his own hand, '34th reading'. Even now I can hardly believe that he read the New Testament 34 times. But knowing the integrity of the man, I cannot doubt it either. And so, one obvious question is, why he was reading the same script so many times.

I like to think that he was trying to make sense of the insanity of the war he had himself participated in. He had been in the Royal Artillery. Was he questioning himself? Questioning the sense of it all? I cannot say. He did not live long enough for me to find out. But a sensitive soul behind a big gun may well wonder what the devastating effects of his discharging repeated salvoes are. Does he hope that they are effective? And, at the same time, does he pray that they are not? I cannot say.

But something motivated my father to read the Bible so many times – always in a quiet place, often to the irritation of others who no doubt wished he would make better use of his time. Yet the impression he made on me was positive, deep and lasting. For here was a man who assumed nothing, who took nothing for granted, who questioned the motives of others, and scrutinised his own infinitely more. In other words, my father was a rare man indeed.

Our house did not have a library, not even a poor one, and although, after his passing, I discovered an old leather suitcase full of books, they were mostly Bible commentaries. What happened to them all, I cannot say. The only book that has come to me from his collection is Bunyan's *Pilgrim's Progress*, which I believe is extremely suggestive, for the author was also struggling to find hope in a world where clear and sufficient grounds for it are woefully scarce. I should like to think that my father and Bunyan were much in agreement concerning the sentiment expressed at the end of that book: *Be ye watchful, and cast away fear; be ye sober, and hope to the end.* (The sobriety mentioned here is not of course that related to the consumption of alcohol, though it might be worth mentioning that my father was teetotal – not an easy feat in a world that invites sensitive souls to strive for a permanent state of self-imposed intoxication.)

There are people who hardly read at all, and most people who read do so for entertainment in one form or another. People read for information or for thrills. The idea that people read to 'improve the mind' seems to belong to some mythical past. Somerset Maugham once made the apparently obvious remark that how and what a writer writes shows the kind of man he is. Something similar might be said of those who read. It seems to me that my father read, at least in part, some kind of divine reassurance – perhaps the reassurance that the kind of inhumanities he had experienced would never happen again. He read to find something comforting, to find the kind of consolation that he could not find from men. In any case, he read reflectively – as he read, he thought. Reflective reading, especially of a philosophical kind, is not so common, no doubt because thinking is considered hard and therefore painful, not to say impractical and irrelevant and so best avoided as much as possible, which strikes me as a rather serious indictment. Reading reflectively requires time and patience, as though the book you are holding deserves the respect some people give to Ming vases. If you deem it undeserving, you might think less of it should it be dropped – like a counterfeit piece of ceramics. Reading of a kind my father was engaged in requires the kind of patience you might give to a poem, and all your attention. One poem at a time, one stanza at a time. And yet, I have heard people openly boasting that they have two or three different books on the go each night, reading several pages of one and then turning swiftly to the next, as though it were a speed contest. I wonder if they can remember what they have read, let alone form an intelligent opinion. There is of course room for reading of all kinds, as there is for music of all kinds, but it strikes me as a tragedy if no room is left for so-called 'serious' music, and no room for the kind of thinking that helps us to find ourselves.

The image I have of my father is partly a consequence of what and how he read. Bespectacled in a quiet corner, legs crossed, an intense expression on an intelligent face and a pipe gently releasing the aroma of Virginia Flake. He lived as he read, quietly and thoughtfully, never raising his voice in anger, a momentary stare from his penetrating blue eyes sufficient to reproach the misdemeanours, rare I hasten to add, of his small son.

I might add in passing that although my parents were happily married, my mother was about 14 years younger, and this, together with the fact that she had had, together with the rest of the domestic population, no experience of battlefield warfare, would have made it difficult for her to understand the weight of his memories. Despite a lack of domestic tensions and wrangles, they were in many respects ill-suited to each other. Marrying at 20 a man who had seen so much, and young enough to want to taste, if not the world, at least those parts of it that they could afford on such a slim salary, it was not the most auspicious of beginnings. He would be mildly rebuked for wanting nothing more than to read and smoke his pipe, while she had had early aspirations to become a ballroom dancer – which she might well have done under different circumstances. She wanted, like most young and attractive girls, to dress up, make new friends and see different parts of her little world. Instead her marriage turned out to be that form of domestic bliss that borders on boredom and atrophy.

With the passing of my father, the marriage was relatively short-lived. My mother understood immediately that, for all his perceived shortcomings, she had lost a rare and goodly man. Her appreciation of him is attested by the profound and unrelenting grief and depression she suffered following his demise. In the years that followed, her spirits approached nearer those much-vaunted sunny uplands, but she never forgot him and he always occupied first place in her heart. Such was the effect he had on her that, since he had died on an evening in early December, every Christmas thereafter was, despite her very best efforts, barely tolerable. When the clock struck midnight on the 25th of every December she would say, 'Thank God it's over for another year.' Tears and Christmas were inseparable companions.

Further evidence of her grief was what, for a considerable time after his death, greeted me on arriving home from school. I would find her sitting on the floor in the living room, surrounded by photographs of my father and striving to wipe away her tears, knowing that I would be opening the door at any minute. I realised that for both our sakes this could not go on, but concluded wrongly that the best thing to do was to destroy the photographs in the fire. This was a schoolboy's solution to an instance of prolonged grieving, and one that I have regretted bitterly ever since. I should have hidden the photographs away instead of depriving my mother and myself of the few material reminders we had left of my father. He was shown in some of the photographs with horses, and his love of them might explain why he was happy to christen me 'lover of horses' – either that or he was thinking of one of The Twelve. Anyway, the burning of the photographs was met with neither protest nor resistance. I guess she was finally approaching a kind of burnout, an exhaustion of grief, and in a spirit of resignation allowed me to do what I thought was best.

One photograph somehow miraculously survived - the portrait which is the title and the inspiration of this whole narrative.

The significance of my father's marriage in this narrative is this: that the love he had for my mother and her own natural sensitivities could not have delivered the balm that my father must have craved after his first-hand experience of war. His feelings were hardly unique, but I believe they went as deep as ever they did or could for anyone else, and deeper than they did for many.

4

THE CONTAGION OF COURAGE

People who read need language to do so. The importance of language is in danger of being underestimated even by those who would give it the highest possible ranking in human life. What concerns me here is the abuse of language and its deterioration, and I believe my father helped me take a stand against it.

My father once took me with him to his place of work, a bus depot, I think to submit a rota or some such piece of paperwork. Yes, he drove buses, for a most meagre living. The room we entered was full of drivers, sitting around, smoking, chatting, and I was a small child, but old enough to remember what happened next. He sat me on a chair and asked me to wait while he did what he had to do. Just then he heard the f-word. He turned sharply and said, 'Don't use words like that – a child is present!' A hush suddenly descended in that room, followed by a perfectly sincere apology. The atmosphere remained subdued until my father returned and we left together hand in hand.

Clearly, I have never forgotten the incident. I have since thought that all present must have respected him, although he was simply one of them, outranking none of them. I also often wonder what would happen today in a similar situation. Would he receive an apology or be sent to Coventry with a flood of abuse and quite possibly a sock on the jaw?

We cannot assess the importance of language, or indeed of anything else, without using it, and that is suggestive of its essential fundamentality. But language can be abused and it can deteriorate, like a muscle that is underused.

For example, understanding the humour in any particular language, if it is verbal humour as distinct from purely visual or slapstick humour, depends on the level of understanding of that language, and the level of understanding in turn depends on the degree of knowledge of that language, the knowledge of grammar structure, pronunciation, and lexis (nouns, verbs, adverbs, adjectives, idiom, and so on). The less the language is understood, the more the understanding of humour will be limited to slapstick, or we might say 'verbal slapstick'. Comedies and comedians, for example, would be judged good or bad on the basis of slapstick or, at best, verbal slapstick, if the nuances of the language are not understood or are misinterpreted.

Gaining a sufficient understanding of a foreign language to enable the learner to understand the nuance, the variety of intonation and the lexis with which verbal humour is a formidable task. It is easy to see how a non-native speaker of a language can miss out on political satire and the more 'informed' forms of humour. As distinct from this, he would have no difficulty appreciating the reaction to someone who slips on a banana skin, or who says 'yes' when asked what the time is.

What about native speakers of the language? And how should children be taught it?

It would be eccentric to say the least if someone should advocate the banning of strong expletives like the f-word. Even the vicar of the parish should be forgiven for using the strongest expletives if he hits his thumb with a hammer while hanging a picture on the vicarage wall. In fact, it would be an interesting joke should he exclaim 'Oh, dear me!' or 'Oops-a-daisy!'

In my father's day, the f-word would never be uttered on television or radio and never seen in a piece of writing. Strong expletives were used when the occasion demanded it, but not as a matter-of-course. His objection to the use of the word in the incident I have described was that it should not be used in front of small children, because it would set the wrong kind of example, and that it should not be used when unnecessary.

It is clear, therefore, that he would be appalled by the standards of today, when the f-word is used willy-nilly, heard routinely on both the small screen and the big screen, and used as almost every other word in casual conversation. I suppose he would say that this suggests an impoverishment of the language, that the very *frequency* in the use of the f-word is itself a form of abuse – an abuse of the language, or, in more modern parlance, a 'cancellation' of the language in favour of, again at best, a form of verbal slapstick. As in so many other areas of life, it is not the use of the f-word that is in question, but the *degree or extent* to which it is used irrespective to suitability, context or appropriateness. It is as though you drove your car at a particular speed irrespective of the circumstances or driving conditions, or as though you painted the front door of your house every year whether it needed to be painted or not and for no reason. If you drive your car in this manner, you are likely to have an accident; if you paint your front door needlessly, you will at least waste money, and probably acquire a reputation for eccentric behaviour; if you use the f-word willy-nilly, it is likely to become quite meaningless, like an exclamation mark inserted at the end of every sentence, while at the same time it will earn you disrespect for your refusal to use the language less abusively, especially in the company of children, impressionable teenagers and more sensitive souls. Cancelling culture, thereby cancelling history, thereby ignorantly and pretentiously throwing the baby out with the bathwater has an effect upon a nation that may be compared with drawing the oxygen out of a room and leaving a vacuum.

The effect on young children is obvious. They will accept the use of the f-word as a norm, to be used whenever and wherever. They believe it 'cool' to follow their adult heroes who so often give publicity to the use of strong expletives. They may jump at the opportunity to impoverish their native language, because, after all, it is infinitely easier to repeat the same simple word than to learn alternatives – to learn alternatives they will need to read 'serious' books, or at least books in which the f-word does not appear on every page, and reading is seldom encouraged by pop culture in favour of violent video games.

Unfortunately, bad examples are contagious, and perhaps it is much easier to follow a bad example than a good one, especially if one is charmed by hero-worship of the lesser 'gods' of our time, but, fortunately, good examples are contagious, too. My father was courageous to object to the use of bad language used in the presence of a small child. He gave me an example of moral courage, and also of integrity, for his integrity gave him the courage to speak out. By extension he also taught me the importance of setting a good example to others, young or old, concerning the use of good judgement in the use of language.

'Culture' is a difficult word, for the concept it denotes is complex. It has become fashionable in some quarters to want to 'cancel' the word altogether, but in favour of what has not been made at all clear. One Italian writer whom I much admire refers to 'God Almighty Culture', intending the phrase to be deeply disparaging. True, the word is like an old hat which has been worn by so many different heads that it has become shapeless. Even so, I should like to cut through this Gordian Knot in the simplest of terms, catching perhaps the most popular understanding (or *mis*understanding!) of the concept, and I am painfully aware that in doing so I risk sacrificing significance on the altar of simplicity, but for reasons of space there is little alternative.

For example, the culture of a nation is bound up with its history, but the history of a nation cannot exist without language insofar as it cannot be recorded and therefore cannot be known and therefore cannot be remembered and therefore cannot be discussed and therefore cannot be learned from. Orwell was well aware of this when he wrote about doublespeak and the manipulation and elimination of history through the doctoring and destruction of written records.

Nuances of language express nuances of feeling and of thought. If you 'cancel' the expression of nuances, you also cancel nuances of feeling and of thought. Feeling and thought lose sophistication through an inability of expression. Human feeling and thought become simpler and perhaps faster, but at the expense of all nuance. It would be a retrogressive step, constituting a downward mutation in human thought and feeling. Reasoned reflection and discussion would suffer, simply because the instruments of reason, the sophistication of thought and feeling, would be in decline.

The ability to express 'nuances', as I have called them, requires that language, although a vibrant and developing phenomenon, should preserve its dignity and variety of expression, while allowing for a certain degree of rebelliousness, just as 'classical' music should be given pride of place over popular music, and why the best that popular music has to offer should be given first place over the worst. Experiment by all means, but don't blow up the laboratory!

None of this is snobbery, 'cultural' or otherwise, and yet there is a certain kind of attitude that holds that speaking your native language correctly must mean showing off. It is interesting that this tendency is less marked when speaking a foreign language – you are congratulated if you appear to be speaking another language very well, and frowned upon if you speak your own with even greater competence. It is almost a contempt for the familiar, or as though you should be scolded for not knowing better, or as though you should wear your old gardening clothes whatever the occasion. Pride in your own language doesn't even get a look in.

The use of language can elevate, or it can ruin reputations. Parliamentary debates are compared to feeding time at the zoo when politicians lose their composure and their command of language with it. The effect of a gradual decline in the quality of language and a consequent decline in the ability to make appropriate and sometimes fine distinctions can stultify political debate and reduce otherwise intellectual debate to a mere grunting match. Statesmen, as distinct from politicians, usually have something to say worth listening to. Politicians evade questions and gorge themselves on a safe diet of cliche and platitude.

But as Orwell knew, the simplification of language in general can itself be a political tool deployed to disable criticism and stifle opposition. If you fake history, you fake culture, too. Accepting what you are told becomes the norm, just as the f-word becomes the norm in the absence of alternatives; and it is infinitely easier to accept what you are told as gospel, just as it is easier to accept the framework than to question the framework itself. A nation of robots is not preferable to an educated electorate, but education begins with language and cannot proceed without language, nor can it reach greater heights without language and further refinements within it.

To live in such ways that change language, for example to change the balance between good and bad language in favour of the latter, is an extremely dangerous matter. A society that allows strong expletives like the f-word to play a large part through its social media and communications network is not providing a benefit to its people. Moreover, such changes may be driven by a tendency to cancel the culture of a country, a tendency which fails to recognise that if you cancel the culture, you must cancel the history, and with that the identity of the nation, with nothing of worth, I might add, to take its place. The tendency to cancel a culture fails to recognise the difference between the baby and the bathwater which it seeks to throw away. A society that abuses its own language abuses itself, for it is terms of language that both the baby and the bathwater exist at all. If this seems obscure, the obscurity is inevitable, for the language of a nation and the culture of a nation are inextricably linked and impossible to disentangle. In other words, it makes no sense to speak of culture and of history as distinct from language.

Language takes a turn for the worse through neglect and

carelessness engendered by an education system that refuses to put *standards* first and marketed by a social media which ignores them; language is protected, preserved and enriched by an education that promotes protection, preservation and enrichment. It follows that we should look after education if we wish to look after our language. The idea that standards don't matter a jot as long as the message gets through is perverse, since it refuses to understand that the quality and clarity of the message depends precisely on the quality and clarity of the language. Sloppy language, sloppy message – and invariably no message at all, or, at least, not the one that was meant. We may not mean what we say, but we should always strive to say what we mean. If *anything* goes, *nothing* goes.

There is sometimes a similar carelessness in the teaching of English as a foreign language. There are those who insist on teaching 'bad language' to foreign learners, because bad language exists and non-native speakers should know about what exists. Quite right. But that is not to say that bad language should receive any kind of primacy in their burgeoning acquisition of lexis. Crime also *exists*! Yes, it's hard to learn new lexis, since there is so much of it and a lot of it is multisyllabic, but the difficulty belongs to the territory – dispense with the difficulty and you dispense with the territory! Students of the language should know the f-word, but they should not be encouraged to use it when there is a treasury of alternatives.

All my talk about the importance of standards is not to be confused with the promotion of either social class or social niceties. I could never feel comfortable having sherry and tea cakes with the vicar or afternoon tea and cucumber sandwiches with the local Women's Guild. I object to neither the vicar nor the Guild and even less to the beverages and the food. But such occasions are just not for me. They are precisely the kind of events for which social niceties are keenly observed, and that's fine, if that's your thing. And I recognise occasions when the strongest possible expletives and combination of expletives would be appropriate.

No, my emphasis on standards has much more to do with empowering people by empowering their minds. Every effort should be made to do this through education, for it is in education where standards should be most clearly explained, expressed and practised. A genuine democracy should be an enabling phenomenon. It should be one in which as many people as possible are enabled to participate, and to truly participate they should understand and assess the choices available to them. A democracy which happily presides over an uneducated electorate is a misnomer and is undeserving of respect. A democracy of ignorance is or ought to be a contradiction in terms. Genuine, meaningful participation in a democracy therefore requires an understanding of what is put forward, and an ability to critically appraise policy, claim and counterclaim, all of which is usually couched in ever-increasing complexity of ideas and almost invariably of lexis. The very least that can be expected from an informed electorate is that it should comprehend the language used.

'One grunt for yes, two grunts for no' is the little we expect from the animals of Orwell's creation. We expect far more from humans, which are, we must continue to think and to hope, quite a world apart. The simplification of language that we find in Orwell's dystopian world is the antithesis of political participation: the simplification of language begets the simplification of ideas, and the simplification of ideas makes fools of us all. Remembering Churchill's assessment, not altogether tongue-in-cheek, that democracy is the worst form of government apart from all the rest, democracy may be defined as the freedom to vote for a species of tyranny, fiscal or otherwise, not simply because the government elected may not be the one you voted for, but because all governments are apt to employ the stratagems of deceit, betraying even those who joyfully voted them into office. An educated, mindful, critical and watchful electorate is essential if a so-called democratically elected government is not to undergo a sliding and sneaky metamorphosis, becoming a tyrannical beast and subjugating the very people it was meant to serve. A newly elected government might consider itself a government 'of the people' dedicated to the righting of all social wrongs and to the delightfully hazy and invariably confused principle of 'equality for all', but if its policies are grounded on a surfeit of righteous indignation, both rich and poor, young and old, and the good and the bad are likely to suffer from its misguided sense of 'justice' and the perverse enthusiasm that drives it. 'Justice' and 'compassion' are not synonymous, neither are 'law' and 'right'.

It seems to follow from much of what has been said so far that people of all ages should be encouraged to read. To say that they should read good books begs an obvious question. Whatever 'good' is taken to mean, it should at the very least mean books written in a language that enriches the reader's knowledge of the lexis of the language – and, I should add, helps feed the critical faculty as well as providing a level of enjoyment. Platitudes are generalisations and generalisations are contentious. In general, however, it may be agreed that writers can be role models for the written word, to be emulated as distinct from imitated.

As a general socio-cultural observation, bitter disappointment, disillusionment, resentment, a sense of personal rejection and hopelessness can all cause a feeling of dismissal of the value of reading, just as it can cause a degeneration in the use of language and an increased frequency in the use of 'bad language' and strong expletives. This may be compared with occasions when we say of someone, 'He's let himself go' – because he's neglecting his appearance and his personal hygiene. A general collapse of personal standards may be compared with a general collapse of impersonal standards. After all, a nation is, amongst other things, the sum of the individuals that compose it. A nation that has abandoned itself to a sense of disillusionment and hopelessness would be expected to pay little attention to the possibilities of linguistic enrichment and the exercise of the critical faculties – what is the point in criticising things that are beyond any hope of repair? (A teacher whose brief was to teach poetry to underprivileged youngsters in a school in a rundown city borough complained that Shakespeare could have no place amongst young people with empty bellies and an understandably strong inclination to rebel against all authority, against all approved standards, including the highest standards of literary composition.) What about the simple act of reading for pleasure? In one screen version of *Moby Dick*, a half-crazed and deeply tormented Captain Ahab stood on the deck of his ship and was about to light his pipe when suddenly he violently tossed it overboard exclaiming, 'Ah, what have I to do with such pleasures!' Whether punk music and rap are also forms of rejection and abandonment, I happily leave the reader to contemplate.

We have come a long way from the incident I described, when my father objected to the f-word used in my presence as a child. I am not saying that my father would have agreed with everything I say in these pages. Not at all. In any case, his early demise deprived me of every opportunity to find out. In fact, I myself often change my mind from one day to the next, lacking as I do the kind of self-confidence that would enable an athlete to achieve Olympian status. I must learn to rest content with my poor abilities. But this much at least is true: that the memory of what happened in that bus depot has been the catalyst of all that I have said. More precisely, it has provided me with a relentless motivation to ask questions, for example questions about the importance of language. I permit myself the liberty to quote from what I have said elsewhere, 'To say, as I have been tempted to say, that language *is* human life, is incorrect; but to say that it is *part* of human life is a profound and widely misconceived understatement'.

I am not forgetting, of course, how that incident showed me an instance of courage and the integrity that inspired it. My father had the courage of his convictions. Sons do not always follow their fathers – a fact for which we may be grateful in many cases, and a fact which we may regret in many more. But he did me the vital service of *showing* me what courage *is*, what moral courage is. He did not attempt to give me a verbal definition, even if there is one. Courage, like love, like integrity, are shown. You might say that he gave me an *ostensive definition* of courage and integrity while at the same time prompting me to ask questions, definitions and questions that have followed me all through my life.

And for this I am eternally grateful. I owe him a debt that can never be repaid in full. But my gratitude does not end here. He taught me something about faith, about hope – and also about acceptance.

5

LESSONS FROM THE HEARTH

My father was sitting on the hearth, with his back to the warm oven when, one day in December, he taught me a lesson that I have consistently failed to grasp, and one that even now, like most other humans, I can understand grudgingly.

'Only seventh, though, Dad,' I said, as I handed him my school report. 'Seventh in the class? Well that's fine. I wish I had been seventh in my day. Well done!' and then he added, 'Do your best – you can't do better than that.' That's all he said. He didn't come up with the usual cliches used by fathers who think it's a good idea to push and squeeze. He didn't say 'Well, there's room for improvement', or 'You can do better'. Much less did he say 'You must do better than this!' or 'I hope you do better next time' or 'You'll have to do better than this if you want to get on!' The time would come when I did do much better, but it was long after he had died, and wasn't because he had pushed me but because I had pushed myself. When I showed him that report I believe that it was with a certain ambivalence, a mixture of self-satisfaction and discontentment on my part. I felt sorry that I hadn't done better, but glad that I hadn't done much worse in a class of about 30.

He wanted me to be the best, but the best *I* could be, not the best *someone else* could be. I must compete with myself and not against others. Competition with yourself must precede competition with others, whether the latter follows from the former or not.

His reaction pleased me and put me at ease. It would be very nice to do better, but it was also nice as far as it went. His reassuring attitude did not come from a lack of academic interest or competence on his part. On the contrary, he helped me with mathematics, giving examples of how equations should be worked, and he did this gently, clearly and patiently. He famously wrote a love poem for my mother during Hitler's war, and kept a notebook full of jottings and reflections. I remember the book had a hard, blue cover and was somehow lost after his demise – a loss I have bitterly regretted. He had left school at 14 and joined the Royal Artillery. I often wonder what he might have achieved had he enjoyed higher education, but in all things theoretical and practical he was self-taught, which is much to his credit.

His reaction to the school report strikes me as a refusal to put me under unnecessary pressure. But the lesson has a physical and atmospheric context, and context and lesson are inseparable.

The occasion of the report meant that school was over for the Christmas holidays, and Decembers then were, I believe, whiter than they have been since. The red coals were giving off their heat in the fireplace and my father was sitting with his back to the warm oven adjacent to it when I handed him that piece of paper, upon which he got up from the hearth and sat on the armchair close to the fire. It was his habit to warm his back against the oven whenever the fire was lit – perhaps the years he had spent in India had accustomed him to heat and over-sensitised him to British winters.

This image of him sitting on the hearth is separable from the lesson I say I still find hard to grasp, namely that, on the one hand, I should strive to be the best that I can be and, on the other, that I should rest content with who and what I am. Perhaps the paradox can be explained like this, that we must endeavour to reach our potential if we are lucky enough to know what that potential is, but it is a matter of indifference whether the result is better or worse than what others can do – having done all we can do, we must rest content with what we have, because it is useless to struggle over what we cannot do. If you are learning to play the cello, you should strive to play better tomorrow than you do today and better still in the days to come; but if you never manage to play like Casals, you must learn to be content with what you can do.

The image of the hearth is what prompts me to remember that day in December. I believe I have been helped to shake off the insatiable desire to be better than anyone else, as though 'being better than anyone else' is a more valid aspiration than continual self-improvement. I say 'helped to shake off', but I do not claim to have succeeded – that would take a better man than I. My father gave me a lifeline when faced with the pressure to step over the heads of others – no father can do better than that, and it's no fault of his if it has tended to slip from my grasp more often than not.

What prompts me to form an image of the hearth is of course the portrait on the landing – an association of ideas that is obviously lost to everyone else. It is as though those eyes, which I know to have been blue, are telling me to slow down, take things easy and not be over-impressed with the doings and achievements of others but to set my sights on my own goals, and to focus less on the splinters in the eyes of others and recognise the shortcomings in my own – sobering advice, not easy to keep in mind in the rough and tumble of life, but reminiscent of W.H. Davies's 'What life is this if, full of care, we have no time to stand and stare'.

As an important side note, this whole idea of being content with what I am after having pushed as hard as I can against my own limits is an essential part of getting to *know* what I am. And happy is the man who knows what he is and remains content with his lot. I say 'what', not 'who', because the issue is not to establish personal identity. The word 'who' only misrepresents the issue, for the issue is to be content with what you are. If you want to act and you are acting then you are happy with what you are. If you want to paint and you are painting then you are happy. Self-fulfilment is the issue. If you are unfulfilled, you are unhappy. 'Know yourself' is not a suggestion that you should check your birth certificate. 'Find yourself' does not mean that you should check your location. Mark Twain found writing, or writing found him, and that was his ticket to self-fulfilment. J.B. Priestley once remarked that he would have written books even if they had earned him nothing. That was his fulfilment, though of course he also enjoyed the pecuniary benefits. I should like to think that Twain and Priestly were in competition with themselves and not with other writers. Wittgenstein on his deathbed said that he had had a happy life, which surprised some people who knew him. His happiness consisted, one supposes, in the fact that he was doing what he wanted to do, namely philosophy. Lack of fulfilment breeds resentment, envy, jealousy, a sense of failure and of alienation.

Finding yourself, finding what you are and therefore what you should be doing, requires a certain inward reflection and no small degree of honesty. You don't find out what you are by asking others. That would be like wanting to know the time of day and consulting a horse. There are some things that we must do and can only do by long, hard, searching self-interrogation. It's sad that so many young people must consult a 'careers officer' in the attempt to find out what they are.

Is everything I have said correct in my reasoning? Is my reasoning flawless? It would be disappointing if it were. There is always room for questions and disputation, the making of distinctions between one thing and another. There is always room for argument and contestation in everything that is far from obvious, and it is always possible, on further reflection, to change your mind, as I frequently do mine.

My father did not give me my reasoning. How could he have done when I was so young and incapable of any serious contribution to discussions of complex matters? It is not my reasoning, valid or defective as it might be, that I owe to my father. What I owe him is my desire to reflect, to think, to ask questions, to dispute – and this is an inestimable gift. It stems from what he was and the image of what he was as a pensive, thoughtful human being, as someone who was searching for answers, of some confirmation, perhaps, of his own values, someone who was in dire need of some reassurance in a world of turmoil, hatred, cruelty, death and destruction.

I owe him my desire to think. And there is so much to reflect upon apart from the myriad minutiae of everyday life that seem to occupy our minds relentlessly. On the downside, man's persistent inhumanity to man must surely top the list which in its train brings death, loss and grief. Not content with the natural shortness of life, man seeks ways in which to make the time he does have that much shorter and akin to the Hell that some religions still espouse.

Life was different, if only slower, in my father's day. Sunday was a special day, and many called it 'a day of rest', and some thought that that was an opportunity for quiet reflection and a little critical self-assessment. In a letter written at the end of the 18th century, William Wilberforce, best remembered for his great stand against slavery, once remarked, 'Oh, what a blessed thing is the Sunday, for giving us an opportunity of serious self-examination, retrospect, and drawing water out of the wells of salvation.' He would be upset to see that now that kind of Sunday is less than a shadow of its former self, for it is simply one day amongst others, for most of us even busier than a 'workday', and has therefore lost its significance as a day that should be a welcome contrast to every other, a day indeed of necessary repose. Of course, even when Wilberforce made that remark, it was as much a comment on the kind of man he was as on the day itself. Still, it would not surprise me if much of his moral diatribe and revulsion against the institution of slavery came to him on a Sunday. Much else might come to us on a Sunday if only we could take a step back from ourselves and our robotic and stultifying pandering to life's pedestrian minutia of routine.

Slavery is of course still very much extant, and it takes many forms. Since Wilberforce, time has been reinvented and is now a monster to which we are enslaved. Before wristwatches, there were pocket watches, hidden away until taken out and leisurely consulted, then these were replaced by wristwatches, which could be consulted much faster, and now there are smart-phones, which control so many aspects of our lives, and time is now only one monster amongst others which are paraded on-screen.

Similarly, weekends are as busy and as fraught as any weekday. I have noted, much to my displeasure, that Saturdays are good days for the receipt of utility bills and tax reminders. It may be true that there is not rest for the wicked, but the good hardly have a better time of it.

For my father, Sunday was the only respite from labour. I remember my mother telling me, 'Your father works every hour God sends him.' This was meant as praise, more for my father than for the Almighty. My father would spend part of his Sunday in chapel, perhaps praising The Lord for the hours of work given him. For my part, I would blame not God but necessity for the slavery to which my father was subjected. It was a question of giving unto Caesar that which is Caesar's. Despite all his efforts we lived on a pittance. Mothers tended not to work in those days, and, in any case, my mother was continually unwell and therefore unfit for the challenges of such forms of slavery. So much for *Arbeit Macht Frei*. Sundays, however, were sacrosanct, and the labours of the factory were replaced by the 'wells of salvation'. Caesar had been appeased, and on Sunday it was God's turn. Nowadays, of course, Caesar holds full sway and there is nothing that is not his.

6

COLD, DEEP, DARK WATERS

Given the restraints of leisure time, it must have been a Saturday or else a most unusual Sunday when my father decided that a trip to the seaside would be a good idea. Buying a car of his own was out of the question and public transport was to say the least awkward, so he borrowed a car for the day, and off we went, stopping on the way for an ice-cream. I suppose I was about seven or eight.

The weather was characteristically grey, windy and far from warm as he parked the car a stone's throw away from the pebbly beach. This was not a good day for lounging on the sand and building sandcastles. But a short paddle ankle-deep wasn't out of the question – after all, we'd come too far to omit it, and doubtless it might be a very long time before such an occasion would arise again.

But my father had something else in mind. Whether he had planned it or whether, as I suspect, it came out of the blue, he decided to give me my first swimming lesson. I suppose the first thing was to accustom me to the feel of water and rid me of the fear of drowning. We were in shallow waters, any shallower and we would have been obliged to paddle. 'Just lie back,' he said, 'I'll hold your head – don't worry – you'll just float – you won't drown, I've got you.' But it was no good. I just jumped up. He tried more gentle persuasion, but he could see that it was useless and gave up. In an instant he seemed to vanish. As I rubbed the water out of my eyes with a towel and turned round, he had swum out to sea, already a mere speck on the horizon, and I feared he might drown. He must have been a strong swimmer. He walked up the beach smiling, towards the car where my mother and I were waiting. Perhaps he wanted to show me what I myself might be capable of if only I trusted myself – if only I had trusted *him*. But, typically, there was no further talk of first principles, let alone a lecture on the importance of learning to swim as a life lesson. I'm quite sure my father had learned to swim as a boy, but I have often wondered how his experience during the evacuation at Dunkirk had depended upon his ability to swim, or at least on the absence of fear of water.

I regret not trusting my head in his hands in those shallow waters. I think my refusal had much more to do with the fear of the water than any lack of trust I had in my father. Fear of water, of the sea, of deep, dark, cold water, has never left me and never will. I have heard of the fear of tunnels or of tube stations, or of heights, or of standing close to the edge of railway platforms, or fear of the dark and of confined spaces. I do believe I am claustrophobic, but the fear of the sea trumps that, and I have never been able to rid myself of its terrors, real or imagined. Fear is the underlying factor, as it is in so many facets of life. My father was sensible, but also brave. As for myself, I have lived life like one invited to a firework display, but who stands so far back that he is unable to see it and is therefore incapable of enjoying the spectacle.

(On the subject of water and towels, my father's advice still rings in my ears every time I take a shower: when drying yourself off, don't use a towel at first, use a flannel instead to take off the excess water, then finish off with a towel – that way, your towel stays fresher for longer. It's strange, how details stick in your memory and which are, very often, more accurate than the larger edifice's our memory constructs.)

I suppose it was only some few years after the trip to the seaside, that the subject of fear raised its ugly head again and was once again related to water, this time the water that pours from the skies.

My father and I were in the garden at the rear of the house. I was no doubt playing about while he was tidying up the garden shed. And then it rained. The rain poured from the sky in buckets. True, I saw the rain through the eyes of a child, but I don't think I've seen it rain so heavily since that time. My father and I looked out from the doorway of the shed. Perhaps he sensed my fear. We stood there watching the rain fall like arrows, and, when it eventually stopped, my father pointed up to a rainbow, 'There, you see? That's God's promise that the world will never be flooded again.' So, there it was. Quite simple. It might rain cats and dogs, but the world will never be flooded again. God said so, and the rainbow was our reassurance. I probably took this quite seriously, though I find it hard to do so now. For my father, however, that rainbow seemed to be a cast-iron assurance, a divine promise. I have already said that my father did not live long enough for me to pose questions concerning religious fundamentalism. I might have asked him, for example, whether he believed in miracles – miracles of the biblical sort. On such matters, I can say nothing further. Perhaps his reference to the rainbow was just a way of putting a child at ease and not an expression of literal belief. But if I had to choose to come down on one side or the other, I would prefer to think, given what I believe to have been my father's search for divine reassurance after his wartime experience, his reference to the rainbow was not at all figurative or merely romantic.

Fear may be a house of many mansions, but many forms of fear may perhaps be best combated by the moral principles or values that we hold, in that what we value rises above, or enables us to rise above, our fears. Courage, after all, is not the absence of fear, but that which enables us to rise above it. Normally, I would avoid running into a burning house, but, despite my fear of fire, I might still do so in order to save a stranger, and would certainly do so to save a loved one. Regard for the life of another may enable me to rise above the fear of losing my own.

If I really believe that the rainbow is God's promise that the world will never be flooded again, I shall not fear that the rain that falls in buckets will do so, though I may, of course, fear that it will ruin the potato patch that I have so carefully cultivated.

If true, the corollary is also true, that the absence of values that might outshine our fears leaves us at their mercy. Fear of the dark is far greater for those who do not believe in the light, or for those who believe that the light will never or can never come.

If my father truly believed in the rainbow, his was a simple belief with a simple full stop. Compare these two statements:

(1) God loves the good because it is good.

(2) The good is good because God loves it.

Which is the more profound of the two? Perhaps the second, because it provides a simple full stop. 'God loves it' is like a full stop to further inquiry, whereas the first statement still leaves open the question, 'Well, God may love the good, but why is the good, good?' The first statement opens the gates to endless and baffling, not to say worthless, philosophical investigation – if, that is, one believes that 'Why is the good, good?' is not a real question.

The lesson I think I learned from the rainbow incident is that facing life with a set of personal values that enable us to put fear in its place is very difficult, but facing life without such values is suicidal. This is not to say what those values should be. Values are to be acquired, and what they are and how they are acquired may be different for different people, yet perhaps they are held far more in common than we sometimes believe. But then, the principle of the sanctity of human life may seem ubiquitous, yet we are frequently disappointed to find that it is not as universal as we wanted to believe and is merely mouthed and routinely flouted.

And if, as I am tempted to do, I speak of my father's simplicity of faith, of belief, of hope, this is in no way a reproach or criticism. Charles Lamb once gently rebuked his friend Coleridge with the words 'cultivate simplicity, Coleridge. There are no hotbeds in the gardens of Parnassus'. This remark was made in the context of Coleridge's approach to religious belief. The concept of simplicity in this context cannot be countered with the observation that life is complicated, or with the truth that circumstances are complex. The reference to simplicity is not meant to deny the entanglement of facts and the reality that moral principles might need to vie with one another when considering them. Instead, we might understand simplicity to mean something like 'purity of heart' or 'goodness of heart', or, if this phrase seems problematic, the simple *desire* to try to do the right thing, whatever the right thing turns out to be and however short of moral perfection it might fall. 'Trying to be good, according to our own lights' is the least we can expect from human beings, and all we can expect from the human race. 'Good'? Well, whatever else we may throw into the arena of philosophical and ethical controversy, it must start with the assumption of the sanctity of human life, for without that, no moral code is worthy of the name – but even this supposition, as fundamental as I am sure my father would have taken it to be, is far from grounded in the fabric of human intercourse. I feel certain he would have agreed that the principle, if we call it such, of the sanctity of human life and its corollary, namely the emphatic and unconditional repudiation of man's inhumanity to man, is what any religion worthy of the name is all about. Gandhi once remarked to the effect that the Sermon on the Mount is the best that any religion can be expected to offer, everything else being, at best, simply wallpaper dressing. Institutional Christianity has deemed the wallpaper a work of inestimable art and mistaken it for the central message, while other creeds, which merely pass for religion, seem to have little or nothing to say on the message at all. The ethics of major religions are underpinned by the promise of a life eternal, since they are unable to found their gospels on the principle that virtue is its own reward. Imagine someone asking Christ, 'Yes, but what's in it for me?'!

If I had had my father's simplicity of faith I might have learned to swim. The matter was dropped, perhaps in the hope that one day that faith would be tested again and used to good effect. I must confess, that day has yet to dawn. I do not have what I believe to have been my father's quest for reassurance and his faith that what we seek we shall find. But I am eternally grateful to him for the example he set and for his simplicity of soul.

Grappling with these matters in my father's absence and therefore with an inability to question him about his faith, I think it is useful to deviate a little in the next chapter to focus on matters which I feel sure preoccupied him from the end of his war experiences to his own demise.

7

MORBID MORAL METAMORPHOSIS

In the natural world, metamorphosis denotes a change or development towards completion, as when a tadpole becomes a frog or a pupa an insect, or a human foetus becomes a baby, and a baby, through the normal run of phases, becomes adult. Such developments are normal, they are what is supposed to happen, they are what is expected to happen. We do not expect a reversal such that the insect returns to a pupa, the frog to a tadpole, a human adult to a baby. Changes in this context are physical and biochemical and, in humans, psychological.

Moral metamorphosis is different. First, it is uniquely human. And although 'metamorphosis' implies development or change, the development or change can just as easily, and I should say infinitely more easily, go into reverse. The possibility of reversal obliges us to distinguish between progression and progress. Progress implies a development for the better, but progression simply means a change or series of changes which may or may not be beneficial or what we should necessarily expect. The end result of a progression may be most unwelcome, whereas it would be odd to speak derisively of what one genuinely believes to be an instance of progress. Expression like 'So much for progress!' implies a criticism, a reproach, a disappointment or disillusionment concerning what is deemed by many to be an instance of progress but which, in the opinion of the critic, isn't. And this kind of progress is often confined to instances of technological or physical development, like new roads or railway systems which are not in some

42

ways better than the roads or systems they have replaced. But 'So much for progress!' might also be a moral reproach, as when a new block of flats is built in such a way as to endanger the lives of its tenants. The critic might express a moral objection by saying that the new block of flats should not be considered a genuine example of progress. In technology, progress is often defined simply in terms of improvements in speed and efficiency, and if such improvements are found wanting, the criticism that they do not represent progress is valid, but amoral.

Progression may go either way and be either good or bad, welcome or unwelcome, beneficial or disastrous, but still be progression, for progression, as distinct from progress, is simply a development of change or series of changes, and most people would readily acknowledge that a change is not always a change for the better and is frequently a change for the worse.

We muddy the waters by introducing the idea of 'moral progress'. By it I suppose would be meant that humans can become better than they are or better than they were and that they can make laws and establish institutions to prove it. About this I am not at all sure. It implies a generality that seems most dubious. To say, for example, that human beings are better now than they were invites me to ask, 'But who, exactly?' The first world war was said to have been fought to end all wars, but has signally failed. The United Nations has failed abominably to exercise its function as a peacekeeping force, and the less said about religions the better.

I am more comfortable with the more neutral and somewhat less assertive notion of 'progression'. There are changes, and some are good and some are bad. The most sobering thought, I believe, is that human beings, not merely in the particular but in the generality, can be subject to the phenomenon with which I have headed this chapter – a morbid moral metamorphosis. In plain language, human beings can become *en masse* less human and more animal in their moral natures. Circumstances can combine to cause a moral decline so that what we now call, with certain moral reservations, 'human civilisation' can disappear from the face of the earth.

The word 'moral' is troublesome, but there is greater complexity to come. For if we include intellectual honesty and academic integrity under the umbrella of 'moral values', then the reverse progression we are considering will also imply an inability to reason. The outcome may well be a kind of civilisation, but it would not be inhabited by what we now would like to call, despite all the burgeoning evidence to the contrary, 'civilised man'.

Might there be no civilisation at all? On this matter, something anecdotal comes to mind, related to me by the Cambridge philosopher Renford Bambrough. Bambrough, then a young philosophy undergraduate, attended a talk by Bertrand Russell in which Russell was extolling the good things that human beings had achieved in the creative arts, in the intellectual domain and elsewhere. In other words, Russell believed that in virtue of everything positive and good that humankind had achieved, human life was worth preserving and therefore worth fighting for. Human life had an indisputable value. During the question session, Bambrough raised his hand and said, 'But what is so special about human existence? Human beings might be extinguished or they might extinguish themselves, just as the dinosaurs came into being and ceased to exist, and this might be considered a natural process or event.' It appeared that Bambrough was not as impressed by humanity as Russell thought he ought to be. Russell scrutinised him for a moment or two and then commented, 'You're a difficult young man, aren't you?'

Perhaps the point was that you either consider human existence worth preserving or you don't. There is a limit to the kind and degree of argument that you can give in favour of the preservation of humanity.

However, another aspect of this little exchange is the recognition that the progression of human existence can go either way – it can either continue to exist or it can be snuffed out, and it can either improve or it can go into decline. And if decline goes far enough and in a certain direction, humanity can come to an end or cease to exist as we know it – and not simply as we know it, but as we would wish to have it.

Humanity can go either way, better or worse. The direction it takes can be very finely balanced. It was in no way inevitable that Nazism would be defeated in the 20th century, and there is no guarantee that Nazism, in the same or different form or by the same or different name, cannot be victorious in the future. Wars can be won. They can also just as easily be lost. There is no guarantee that humanity can resist both moral and intellectual decline, even to the extent that it can become unrecognisable according to present-day standards or to standards which most people would consider those of a truly civilised race of beings.

It is this extremely tenuous nature of humanity and its direction that interests me and, I believe, preoccupied my father. As a thinking man he fought for freedom as against enslavement, for the sanctity of human life over indescribable inhumanity. But there was despair as well as hope, doubts whether victory was likely or even possible as well as certainty that the fight was winnable. In such a world of contrasts in which outcomes were held in the balance and in which one man's hopes could not possibly influence the course of events, where could he turn for any form of reassurance? Not to man, for man is the very hub of uncertainties. The kind of simplicity that he believed was represented by the rainbow was the only recourse, the only source of reassurance. Such simplicity of faith was the only blade that could cut through the Gordian Knot of doubts and uncertainties, whatever the outcome of events.

This kind of simplicity is a sacred thing. It comes when everything else and everyone else is exhausted and found wanting. Imagine the attempt to live in such a way that when death comes you are ready for it. Difficult? Oh yes! It's hard to imagine anything more demanding. But that is because there is so much that stands in the way, so much that charms us into a multiplicity of illusions. We must first rid ourselves of these, and then what we seek is easier, but not easy, to achieve. An analogy comes to mind.

The summer was long, hot and wet. The amount of growth in gardens seemed unprecedented. October, the lopping and pruning season for many, sees men and women in their gardens attempting to curb the growth; they cut and they prune as though punishing plants, bushes and trees for being so bold. A gardener, armed with a long, hand-held and hand-operated lopping device, tackles the growth but is unable to reach the topmost branches and twigs of bush and tree, even when standing most precariously on the slender platforms atop of ladders and steps. He struggles and even takes his life in his own hands to prune trees and bushes, to cut branches and snip twigs which are just, so tantalisingly, out of reach, outside his reach and that of the implements he uses. He tries again and again, but fails, and finally speaks of the inevitable – of 'the one that got away', and he tries to console himself with the thought that he did the very best he could. Such is the attempt to live in such a way that when death comes knocking, you are more than willing to leave the door ajar. Such is the admirable, for many might say so, but vain attempt to 'learn how to die'.

Simplicity of faith is the very last outpost before the fortress we have built for ourselves is finally overwhelmed and we find ourselves falling with it and despite it or because of it. Simplicity of faith overrides doubts, even of the most lingering kind, but it also overrides hope. It is the kind of acceptance that lies at the bottom of the barrel. My grandmother, whom I remember as though she were a saint amongst saints, would say, quoting the song, 'What will be, will be.' Simplicity of faith demands that we comply fully and totally with the same sentiment.

I might also say that simplicity of faith is or requires a kind of stripping bare, a peeling away of layer upon layer of illusion. Perhaps Lear in the storm was subject to the same debunking, the same removal of illusion and self-deception, the same stripping down to the bare self – 'Come! Off, you lendings! Come, unbutton here!' Interesting that such an awakening arises when all seems lost or all has been lost!

There are things that few know or can even dream of unless they have themselves felt the power of such awakenings, their magic, their enchantment. I recently heard one say that his walks on the so-called 'mountains' of the valleys of South Wales helped him clear his mind. This description of the effect of such places does not even begin to do justice to what they do. They are capable of stripping bare the very soul of those who dare walk in them – yes, these hills, for to call them 'mountains' would annoy the Swiss or anyone who is more impressed by height than by substance. The sense of emptiness you feel in these hills is overwhelming, such that the strong desire to go there is matched by the strongest possible desire to leave.

'Simplicity of faith' is an awkward phrase, and I don't much like it though I have used it several times. I am not at all sure that the experience of the desolate Welsh hills has much at all to do with faith, simple or otherwise. But it does give you, or at least it gave me, a sense of nakedness, or hollowness, as though you are drained of all illusions, of all dreams, of all myths – as though you are given an insight into what death is like, a state of non-being. This might be the beginning of something that can be called a simplicity of faith, a motivation, so to speak, towards it. Or it might just leave you with an insufferable sense of nothingness, which might explain why, after an hour of it, you make to leave it as expeditiously as possible, promising yourself that the experience will not be repeated in the foreseeable future if you can possibly help it.

Like many who had experienced the horrors of war and survived them, my father might have hoped for better times – hoped without expectation. But I doubt whether he entertained any illusions concerning a future utopia and a more compassionate mankind. His hope was perhaps founded on what I have grudgingly called a simplicity of faith. He must have known that the future welfare of mankind could not be guaranteed with rainbows. His beliefs, whatever they were, no doubt helped to sustain him through the war years, and his confidence might have been further buttressed by the fact that, after unimaginable losses of life and tales of unspeakable cruelties and inhumanities, victory was finally given to freedom over enslavement. Even so, victory in war does not of itself offer any guarantees that thereafter human nature will be remoulded and set upon a higher moral pedestal than hitherto. He must have known this. Having experienced some of the worst things human beings are capable of, he must have hoped and prayed that they would not be repeated. But the revelation of the worst that man can do must have been a sobering one, one which sounded a loud note of caution.

But lessons are not learned by all or at the same time, and many pupils leave school without having learned a thing of value.

Primo Levi was sustained throughout his time in the concentration camp by the thought that he must outlive the experience in order to tell the civilised world all about it, as though the telling would prompt everyone to join hands in a moral celebration of the dignity of man and the sanctity of human life. There is little doubt that his being met with boredom and indifference contributed to the sense of futility and despair that caused him to take his own life. It is tragically and suggestively ironic that it was not the concentration camp that killed him but the coldness of the 'civilised' world to which he afterwards desperately appealed. Inhumanity does not end with the ending of wars, it is only that it seems more acceptable, inevitable even, to those who wage wars and participate in them.

Which, I suppose, is why there must have been many who were disinclined to participate in the merry celebrations that took place in Trafalgar Square and elsewhere at the formal announcement of the end of hostilities. There were so many who had lost so much, but also many who, having seen the evil that men do, worried as much about the future as they lamented about the past. And this, no doubt, is the note of sobriety that Bunyan wishes to strike, 'Be ye watchful, and cast away fear; be sober, and hope to the end.'

If I speak of a 'simplicity of faith' concerning my father, I mean to say that he was not impressed with the institutional baggage of religion, with the ritual and the ceremony, all of which supposedly gives gravitas to religious belief and its expression. He was a simple man and would not have been overawed by the wealth of the Vatican, for example.

But the phrase 'simplicity of faith' is far from plain-sailing when it comes to a belief in a loving God. Such a faith is anything but simple. If God is thought to be some kind of superman or super-being, all-knowing and all-powerful and all-compassionate, then the obvious problem is to square this with man's inhumanity to man, with cruelty to children, with the innumerable and unspeakable injustices that make up the human condition.

If, instead, God is thought of as an umbrella term for goodness, for love of humanity and all the righteous principles that follow from this, if God is not thought of as some kind of physical entity, then He cannot be blamed for inactivity or indifference, because there is no one or nothing to blame! Man is the author of his own fate, and whether he indulges his vices and eventually ceases to exist or whether he somehow rises above his animal nature and achieves a morally superior state of being, is all up to him. Something or someone called 'God' doesn't come into it.

This conception of God is not acceptable to most organised or established religions. I doubt whether my father accepted it, either. I also doubt whether he rejected the intellectually monstrous idea of some kind of Hereafter. But this is no slight whatsoever on his intelligence. Why? Because faith is not a simple idea. Faith in God, whether God is thought of as a super-being or simply as a way of speaking of The Good, is like a piece of ceramics – although valuable, it can get knocked about, chips and cracks may appear over time, it is not unbreakable, and the longer it survives the more it is subject to damage, disfigurement and even rejection. The good man is not one who forever lives in a cocoon of absolute certainty. He is beset with doubts and uncertainties in a world which invites precisely this unsettled state of mind. Such uncertainties are not proof of a man's weakness but of his intelligence. He lives, as it were, in a twilight zone, a misty region somewhere between conviction and uncertainty, between doubting and acceptance come-what-may, a rather unpleasant state of ambivalence, the only consolation being that there is just as much chance that good will prevail as that it won't. I am reminded of the misty regions enjoyed by those who speak of time travel, a notion they find at once absurd and yet perhaps possible. And here I am again reminded of how many times my father read the New Testament, reading the same texts over and over again, as though he were searching in a state of uncertainty for some kind of reassurance that would be lasting and impervious to doubt, and never quite finding it. There is simply a limit to what an intelligent man can be expected to take on trust, assuming that what he is expected to take on trust makes sense!

In short, my father was a good man. On the day of his funeral, one of his brothers called me over and said, 'Remember, your father was a good man.' I had rarely seen my uncle before that, and after that announcement I never saw him again. I already knew that my father was a good man and didn't need to be reminded of it. There is a certain simplicity in goodness, but there is no simplicity in the faith of an intelligent man. Faith is complex, and it is as complex as it is burdensome – tossed about and battered as it is by intelligence, wisdom and the stark realisation that a morbid moral metamorphosis is just as likely as a gentle drift towards utopia.

And that I think is all I am entitled to say about my father's approach to religion and the nature of his religious belief, namely that he was a good man. I should like to think that he would have sympathised deeply with Gandhi's remark that The Sermon on the Mount is the very best that any religion can do and that all the rest is, at best, a wallpaper-pattern and, at worst, a series of stumbling blocks.

8

THE PORTRAIT MOVES

Focus on the face in the frame long enough and it will appear to move, the lips, the eyes, almost imperceptibly, almost as though the eyes and the lips and even the cheeks are responding to something that is said or thought – a sort of silent and one-sided conversation. Is this an optical illusion, a trick of the light, or is it purely in the imagination of the one who sees it or thinks he sees it?

This kind of observation might have been a preamble to the kind of ghost stories people insist on writing and others enjoy reading. The reference to movements in the portrait of my father, however, is anything but a setting for a tale of horror. It represents, I believe, a reawakening and a deepening of my relationship with my father, a process that has been taking place over a number of years. It's almost as though my father has become a Lazarus and a fixture in my daily life – as though the two-dimensional portrait has become flesh and blood. I am meeting him again, in a twilight zone where the two-dimensional and the three-dimensional meet.

The process had a genesis in the moment my father died all those years ago. It meant for me a transition from the world of childhood to that of manhood, and the threshold of that new world was pain, the pain of loss, of grief. Perhaps I was reborn in that moment, and rebirth is not necessarily a pleasant thing, but the pain it engenders can bring forth new life, a new conscience, a new vision, a reassessment of the world in which you find yourself.

I do not stand and stare at the portrait, but I wave my hand or nod every time I pass it, as though it were a question of solemn duty, a sight eccentric and even comedic to a casual observer and not the sort of thing you would mention in routine conversation, even if you were stuck for a topic or a funny thing to say.

The face I see in the portrait is naturally engraved indelibly on my psyche – a young face, intelligent, insightful, hopeful, and not at all the face it was to become in the months and weeks before his demise when, though only in his mid-to-late 40s, his complexion was ashen-grey on deeply lined skin and his receding hair was half-white, and his blue eyes seemed dim. I lay awake at night worried that my father was visibly growing older and all too conscious that there was nothing I could do to reverse it.

To say that I lost him when he died and rediscovered him years later would not be right. He was almost lost to me long before that, when I was about ten years old. 'Who do you want to live with?' asked my mother, coldly. 'Me, or your father?' My father had allowed the small joint of beef to burn in the oven which was next to the fireplace. As was his custom, he sat reading with his back to the oven and had totally forgotten to check the progress inside it. Enraged, my mother had complained to my grandmother and my father quickly became a pariah. One thing had led to another and, for a while, the future of the marital union was in some doubt. The whole thing blew over, as such things do, and no doubt the episode of the burned beef was symptomatic of a deeper divide between my parents, one of incompatibility of personality and mindset. But, as already mentioned, when my father eventually shook off his mortal coil, my mother was devastated, never got over it and sang his praises to the end of her days. Love always wins, it seems, at the end of every day. Eventually, the episode took on the character of a family joke, embellished and embossed and treated with the same air of nonchalant humour as King Arthur's burning of the cakes. Yet, it was no joke at the same, certainly not in the eyes of a ten-year-old, who should never suffer the pain of such questions as, 'Who do you want to live with, your mother or your father?'

So, after all that we all continued to live quite happily together, until my father's health visibly deteriorated and to such an extent that the medical diagnosis 'nerves of the stomach' had little credence and therefore gave little consolation being a somewhat contemptuous, dishonest and insulting expression of ignorance. 'Doctors don't know everything,' said my maternal grandfather, a retired plumber. 'If I make mistakes, I must go back and correct them, but they bury theirs.' 'You have to be your own doctor' was the consensus of agreement, a sentiment frequently uttered as a mantra yet seldom acted upon.

The plumber died in hospital and was terribly missed, for my mother and her father were extremely close. My father died at home just a couple of years later, and his departure was devastating despite the gulf of experience and mindset that had separated man and wife, a gulf that was suggested by my father at one time announcing, 'The best songs are hymns.'

The story has it that as a toddler and therefore not knowing any better, I hit my father on the head with a rubber hammer as he was bending down to tie my shoelaces. But much worse was to come when I was about five or six in the form of what we might call a divine embarrassment, and the mention of hymns brings it to mind.

From an early age I was expected to dress up in my finest and accompany my father to chapel on a Sunday. Only one such Sunday stands out in the family chronicle of events. When the congregation sat down after rendering a hymn of praise and in the few seconds that normally lapse between the regaining of composure and the beginning of the sermon, I said in quite a loud voice, 'Dad, they're all bloody mad!' I can only imagine the look of horror on my father's face as he quickly ushered me out of the chapel and took me into the cemetery outside to pick the daisies that grew there. I can't remember what he might have said to people as they left the church later, though I am confident that he would never have attempted to disown me. I had caused him embarrassment, and it was a mystery to all and sundry how well I had managed to pick up a swear word and use it to such 'good' effect. 'You mustn't say things like that!' and 'You mustn't use bad words again!' were probably the things they said to me later. But at that tender age I couldn't have understood the difference between good and bad. I was never punished for my misdemeanour, and, once again, the whole episode became, in the fullness of time, a family joke. Saying what I did probably let me off the hook for a while concerning Sunday attendance at the chapel – some distance was required so that memories might fade and the whole event be shrouded in a handful or two of mist and myth. My father was far from humourless and no doubt the event gave him something to smile about for years to come. Apparently, when one of the parishioners asked my whereabouts. 'Oh, he's picking daisies!' Dad replied. I believe I might have been picking daisies thereafter all my life long, but I make no apologies for that.

I might say, *en passant*, that my infant judgement regarding the insanity of mankind has undergone woefully little revision during adulthood and, by all appearances, remains depressingly sound. Alas, though infant, that judgement was by no means infantile.

Some years later, my father came home from a hard day's work to find that I had been given a rabbit by a friend. The bunny needed a hutch and my father set to work to make one from the bits and pieces of wood and mesh he found in the garden shed. Once completed, the rabbit took up residence and seemed content. Several days passed and, on returning home, my father found that I had acquired yet another rabbit. The existing hutch was too small, and he set about making an extension. He said nothing about greed, but he looked at me disapprovingly. No fuss was made about it and he had set about the task willingly enough, but the whole thing left me with a feeling of guilt for having two rabbits instead of one and for putting my father to so much trouble when he was obviously tired and lacked the proper materials to do a job of housing two rabbits with a construction that was not really adequate. The rabbits were cross with one another, and finally they were returned to their original owner. I believe I remember feeling glad to see them go. The episode had exhausted my father gratuitously though he had risen to the task without complaint.

Without complaint – except for that look of disapproval he had given me on the acquisition of that second rabbit. I interpreted it then and have done so ever since as a lesson in greed, one perfectly consistent with the lesson he gave at the dining table, 'You should leave the table feeling that you could eat just as much again', or 'When thirsty, don't gulp it all down, drink a little at a time'.

Such was my father. When angry or disapproving, it was anger and disapproval in subdued format. He never raised his voice, let alone his hand. I don't remember him saying anything in anger or vitriol. His eyes spoke for him, and what they expressed never lingered longer than it should.

As for the lesson in greed, I cannot claim to have mastered it, and no one would believe me if I said I had, but I flatter myself with the observation that I have done my best to avoid excess and have largely succeeded in doing so. Whenever I have overstepped the mark it has usually been in the nature of a peccadillo. My relatively small collection of tobacco pipes I have called a hobby, and I have fortunately avoided the most common forms of excessive or clinical greed, namely addiction and obsession. If I have wanted to buy more than one of the same item, my father's admonition always comes to mind and feels like a gentle slap in the face, yet it has seldom prevented me from making a gratuitous outlay. I am not perfect and I am happy to own up to my imperfections.

By now it should have become clear that this narrative is as much about me as it is about my father. I can make no apology for this. Apart from the fact that I am in no position to write, and would not in any case wish to write, a biography, the focus is very much the relationship between my father and me as far as it went when he was alive, as it has been since his demise, and as it is now. The portrait moves, and it does so not merely physically, as I have explained at the outset, but also in that it directs my thinking, my reflections, my self-reproach.

For instance, I am several decades older now than my father was when he died, and I feel bound to ask what good I have done with this extra time. I claim to have an idea of what good he did, I mean in the lessons he taught me simply by being the kind of man he was. I must ask myself whether I have succeeded in living up to the mark, and I am not at all confident that I have got anywhere near it. Despite my self-doubt, he provided that mark, one which I believe I have missed time and time again, but at least I have known the mark and, more often than not, have aimed for it, as a mountain climber stretches out to the next hand-hold. How many times I have stretched out, missed the hold and slipped back down I cannot say, but I have never achieved such a height that a fall would see the end of me – such is the imperfection of Everyman, and I can hardly claim to be any better. The power of my father, and hence the power of the portrait, resides in this, that it *contains the mark*!

Not a ghost story, then, when I say that the portrait moves.

But it also speaks.

9

THE PORTRAIT SPEAKS

Yes, the portrait also speaks.

I ask it a question, though not out loud unless I am alone, and it answers inside my head in the voice I remember, or think I remember – that mild-mannered, unhurried, gentle tone, a tone that I find difficult to emulate. Or perhaps it's not a question, just a remark, and it remarks in return.

I find myself apologising to the portrait for all that my father has missed, such that what I say to the portrait seems just as important, or even more so, than what the portrait says to me. I find myself in apologetic mode, apologising for what he has missed by dying so young.

He missed my higher education. Had he lived, we might have walked hand in hand through the corridors, the archways, and beneath the towers of academia, and he might have marvelled at the libraries, the innumerable books and the learned personages bedecked with gowns of distinction who preamble beneath the spires of… Ah, yes, all of this is pure romanticism, of course. Even so, he would have loved to know that his little son had come so far – to know this, and not know how little it is to come so far.

He also missed my marriage, and the birth and education of his grandchildren. And, perhaps above all, he missed time with his wife, the woman to whom he wrote poems from the chaos and the sound and the fury of war. I have found myself apologising for my own weaknesses and shortcomings, so that my father has become my Father Confessor. How many fathers become Father Confessors? How many are blamed for their shortcomings, their weaknesses, their omissions?

It is well worth mentioning here that what some people call 'bonding' between father and son never occurred. There was no such thing, for example, as attending football matches together. I believe, but can't claim to know, that my father had no interest in football. Even if he had, stadiums were not easily accessible without a car, and he had neither the time nor the money necessary to follow a team or take me to watch a game. Holidays in the country for a week or two, or camping together in woodlands, were not on the agenda; again the lack of money and opportunity ruled them out. Moments of togetherness with my father were irregular and infrequent. 'Bonding', if we insist on calling it that, consisted of scraps and crumbs, but, collectively, they were more than sufficient to enable me to form an image of him which, as I am endeavouring to show, was lasting, indelible and eminently worthy of emulation. He was a quiet man, but silence can speak volumes.

A quick snapshot, perhaps when no one is looking or caring, can reveal more than a studied and, almost invariably, unnatural, piece of photographic portraiture. So it is that my memories of my father appear to be anecdotal but most revealing. The budgerigar incident is a case in point, when some family members were engaged in wallpapering the living room. Someone inadvisedly opened Joey's cage. He flew round the room and then decided to perch on the rim of the bucket which contained the wallpaper paste. The poor bird slipped and fell into the paste, an event which most of the company considered most amusing. My father was the only one who retained his composure. 'I see nothing to laugh about,' he said, as he gently lifted Joey out of the bucket and made his way to the bathroom to clean the bird up as best he could. My father's reproach, softly spoken but firm, only raised the laughter further, presumably because my father's solemnity contrasted with the slapstick humour of the event. Joey survived the incident well enough, but, when returned to his cage by my father's solicitous hands, turned his back on the company for the rest of the day.

The incident was told and retold many times thereafter, but what he revealed to me about my father was significant and lasting. He was not a humourless man, but he was prepared to sail against the tide if he thought it right to do so. He was not one of the crowd. He was prepared to do what was right even when 'doing the right thing' was considered amusing or even slightly eccentric. He might have smiled at the incident, but only later, and only in the knowledge that Joey was safe and well. The anecdote speaks volumes of indelible print to me – an invaluable snapshot of the kind of man my father was, and of the kind of man I have in some important respects failed to be.

The portrait speaks these volumes. It is also a source of music. For my father not only stated that hymns were the best songs, he actually played them on an organ as if to demonstrate the proposition. How my parents managed to get that heavy, antiquated and musty old church relic upstairs and into the spare room, I can't imagine. But manage it they did. My father, who was endowed with not a little musical talent, managed to play it very well, and songs of praise filtered downstairs and throughout the house, though I don't recall that he ever actually sang the hymns – he probably felt that the organ was sufficient in and of itself. The organ was loud, but despite a lot of soft-pedalling, the instrument had a short life and was removed – where I can't say, but no doubt to a place of solemn rest far from the house and the whole neighbourhood. I don't know whether this was a response to complaints from the neighbours, but no doubt my mother's own misgivings were more than sufficient to seal its fate.

I remember my father saved up for and acquired a chromatic harmonica (as distinct from a simple mouth organ). He played it with great dexterity. He was a master of rhythmic 'vamping' and included some classic love songs in his repertoire – his rendering of 'Beautiful Dreamer' was particularly memorable and, come to think of it, a title delightfully apt. Far less objectionable to all and sundry than the chapel organ, the harmonica was permitted to remain. My father kept it lovingly in its box in the bottom drawer of the sideboard in the living room. It was one of his treasured possessions.

The bottom drawer of the sideboard is particularly worthy of note, not in itself but for what it contained. The harmonica was not my father's only treasure, nor was it the most treasured. His Bible took first place, and this he kept wrapped in a green, plastic cover, next to the harmonica. He kept his tobacco pipe in that drawer, also. He possessed only one pipe, a small, thin one which had seen better days and which he smoked infrequently, preferring un-tipped cigarettes. When he did smoke it, it seemed to be with a deep, melancholy frown, as though he was desperately trying to work something out. Apart from these three items in the bottom drawer, the only other object which helped to characterise him was an inexpensive pocket watch which he kept on a chain in the top pocket of his jacket.

Mahatma Gandhi comes to mind, for, it is said, after this great man's death, all his possessions could be fitted quite nicely into a shoebox, evidence perhaps of his disrespect for, or lack of reliance on, material wealth and his focus on much higher things. My father had spent some time in India, during, I believe, a period of convalescence, and this is where he had bought a copy of John Bunyan's *Pilgrim's Progress*, a nicely bound edition by Collins, which, I almost forgot to mention, was also kept in the bottom drawer of the sideboard in the living room. Inside the cover he wrote in pencil, 'India Command, Deolali India, 1945'. He did not live long enough to be asked, but I am sure he would have held Gandhi in the highest esteem. It seems to me that the shoebox and the bottom drawer of the sideboard have much in common and say pretty much the same sort of thing.

Needless to say, that little copy of Bunyan's book is now one of my most treasured possessions, and it will hopefully assume a similar status amongst those of my children – I have no doubt that it will.

The power of the portrait is the memories it contains, the images it invokes, and above all the inspiration it engenders, inspiration just as strong as that which invited the toasts to Greek philosophers that were a regular feature of a Saturday night out.

10

THE GREEK PHILOSOPHERS

We poorer students had to make a pint or two of beer last, and this was achieved by saluting ancient Greek philosophers one by one with suitable time lapses between. We might begin with 'Hail to Thales' or 'Hail to Parmenides' and end much later with 'Hail to Aristotle'. The process was repeated if a second pint was affordable. My father might have frowned on my drinking even this modest amount, but he would I think have been pleased to hear the ancients toasted by those who would have been honoured to sit at their feet.

The portrait conjures up an endearing image of my father and I walking slowly arm in arm through the university precincts, remarking now in the architecture, now on the course of my studies, with an 'Oh, that's so interesting' or 'Well, that's wonderful!' I might have asked him about Bunyan's Pilgrim's Progress, which by then I would have read, and he might have coloured his remarks with anecdotes from his war days.

In this way, the portrait has renewed my relationship with my father, or should I say *created* it? The portrait, inanimate in itself, has provided a vicarious relationship with the deceased. Our lives are what they are thanks to the people who have embellished them, not forgetting those, also, who have soured them. Other people make us what we are, and my father at least lived long enough to give substance to a two-dimensional picture of his face. Our little lives, the Bard has said, are

59

rounded by a sleep. Our lives are also shaped by those who sleep and cannot wake, permanently cast in a two-dimensional representation of how they used to be. The dead are not therefore bereft of power. On the contrary, death can confer on them a mantle of power that they never would have achieved when awake. 'The grave's a fine and private place. But none, I think, do there embrace,' says Andrew Marvell. Yes, but there is a kind of life beyond the grave for those who lie there, a life in the lives of those who cannot let them go, who have no wish to let them go, but who, on the contrary, take their very sustenance from the dead, are enlivened by them and inspired by them. Socrates and Plato still live in the lives of those who will not let them go, as my father lives in mine. There is also irony in the fact that the dead may exert a greater power than the living – more power than those who occupy high places and enjoy the adoration, real or fictional, of the masses.

Mention of the ancient Greeks brings to mind a scarcely believable perception which is currently infecting some institutions of learning. It is a view promulgated by some professors and is so limp and dangerously misguided that it cannot possibly be squared with their entitlement to profess anything beyond the banal and the simplistic.

Their view is that the study of ancient Greek philosophy, notably that of Plato and Aristotle, is irrelevant in the modern world and should be replaced by more recent contributions to social and political issues which are more recognisably current and in need of serious debate.

I look to the portrait of my father and his relaxed brow becomes a frown. I'm almost certain I hear him say that to neglect the philosophers of old is like sawing the legs off the dining room table. If you saw the legs off a table, is it still a table? Is it a table without legs, or is it just a round or square or rectangular surface which was once an important part of a table? The matter may be debated, but I shall take it no further here, except to say that it might reasonably be called a 'question of definition'.

There are other kinds of definition. I refer to probity and intellect, especially the latter. If anyone would like to know what intellect is, or what intellectual probity is, or what intellectual honesty is, they could do no better than to read Plato's Socratic dialogues. Plato is not of course the only example, but I doubt very much whether any age has bettered him as an example of intellectual capability and integrity. He is worth reading for this alone. He shows us how to think or what thinking *is*, which is quite different from telling us *what* to think. *What* Plato thinks is obviously debatable, but *how* he thinks is a paradigm example of human intellectual achievement. To read and understand Plato, we must be capable of *following the argument*. Reading him helps to teach us to do this, and debating him helps us to form our own opinions. Aristotle was followed slavishly in the Middle Ages and beyond in many European universities, even to the point of issuing fines to students who disagreed with him. Much of what Aristotle says is now scientifically either false or highly suspect, but this does not mean that he has nothing to offer. I remember being reproached by one of my tutors for attacking statements that I had successfully argued were false. Dismayed, I asked for an explanation. 'A false proposition might still be a bloody good proposition,' he replied, adding that I hadn't taken the trouble to look behind the proposition to understand what had prompted it – I had failed to achieve a 'marriage of minds' with the writer in question. I came to understand that this was a failure of intellect and of imagination.

That is not all, for what *concerns* Plato is timeless and therefore most relevant to us. The subjects that come under his scrutiny are entirely pertinent to this and every conceivable age of humanity, for as long as humanity remains what it is and does not sink into the abyss of irreversible mediocrity and stupefaction, such as politics, education, and the universal and omnipresent question, 'Why should I bother to be good?' In fact to say that Plato is irrelevant is to say that philosophy and philosophical debate are irrelevant, which is a proposition that one certainly does not expect from anyone who professes to teach the young a thing or two.

Plato, and others of his ilk, are landmarks in the history of human thought. A society entirely obsessed with racism and other forms of discrimination are in danger of throwing the baby out with the bathwater when they talk of what is and what is not relevant to contemporary social issues. These issues are important, but they require thinking as well as feeling, and thinking and feeling are bound together inseparably. If thinking is not irrelevant, neither is Plato, who is one of the relatively few paradigms of critical thought.

The proposition that Plato and others are irrelevant is a political judgement of some considerable bias and therefore unreliable and significantly debatable. I feel guilty for making it seem worthy of rebuttal. Such is the fate of such bland propositions, even when what lies far beneath them may after all have some merit. Some merit – and so it does not surprise me to hear a chorus of dissenting voices from those who seek to change society for the better according to their lights, 'We don't disagree with what you say, but today is today and we must act if we want to get anywhere.' To which I can only reply that they must teach people to improve their ability to think and then encourage them to think a lot more before they act. Thinking is hard and therefore unpopular, which is one reason amongst others why society isn't a far better place than it could be. And because thinking is hard, philosophy is reproached for being irrelevant anyway. If philosophy were a sentient being, it would be entitled to protection under the banner RSPCP, being already insanely, cruelly and mindlessly mistreated, because so profoundly misunderstood and cynically misjudged. And as for 'today is today', it should be remembered that today is today because of yesterday and that so often we must take a step back before we move forward, which is why the thinkers of the past have something to tell us – if only we could learn to listen. Perhaps we should be forgiven for thinking that everything began with us and that only now and the more recent past have any real claim to consideration. But such pretensions are the devil and should be resisted. Once again, it is not necessarily *what* they tell us but *how* they tell us that can teach us something about the ability to present a case, to analyse, to think critically. If thinking is hard, it requires courage to undertake. The harder the thinking, the greater the courage required. Perhaps that is what is missing: courage. But courage requires motivation, and the motivation comes from the conviction that thinking counts and must count. Such conviction must be taught, encouraged and exemplified in the works of people like the Greek philosophers who were sufficiently interested in their surroundings to wonder and speculate and suggest and recommend. How to argue, how to think critically, are essential skills. Having said that, young and old alike should also be encouraged to take an interest in what capable people of the past had to *say*. More of profound relevance can be learned from Boethius's *Consolation of Philosophy* or from the *Confessions* of Marcus Aurelius or those of Saint Augustine than from a whole library of contemporary novels or a formidable spectrum of computer manuals. Why is this? Because intelligence is extremely common and wisdom is decidedly not. Wisdom, the handmaiden of love, is an essential precondition of positive social change. If society seems to be on the back foot and if human beings appear to be mutating in a downward spiral, a deficiency of wisdom is invariably the cause. But respect for the works of people like Boethius, Aurelius and Augustine takes time to explain, foster and inculcate, and space must continue to be reserved for creating this kind of sensitivity in our system of education. If, on the contrary, such ambitions prove baseless because there is never space for them on any school curriculum, profundity has been sacrificed on the altar of immediate pragmatism, and humanity is very much the loser. The table has lost its legs and is deprived of any dignity it may have had. It is now merely one small surface amongst so many, and humanity has lost something of itself. Debatable? Certainly. Let us by all means debate, remembering that the force of argument is preferable to the argument of force and that the so-called 'argument of force' is of course no argument at all. Let us first have the tools of argument so that, in Socratic mood, we might 'follow the logos wherever it may lead' and whatever the cost to our puerile prejudices.

It is hard to find anything so wrongheaded as the suggestion that this or that subject of classical study should be crossed off the curriculum and replaced with something we know not what or not replaced at all. The pruning of trees should be undertaken with the greatest care – too much pruning and the tree dies.

I move on. But as I pass the portrait of my father on the landing, I notice the frown has disappeared. His gentle smile has returned, and, if I stay long enough, I might even make out a slight nod of the head, as if to say, 'And quite right, too!' Such, again, is the power my father exudes, encased and two-dimensional though he may be. His reflections (not entirely surprisingly) match my own – or would have done, I should like to think.

If I say that my father is a role model, albeit now two-dimensional and encased in a frame, it's not too surprising that a role model should also be a template against which, consciously or unconsciously, others are judged or measured. In all my long years, John Barker came closest to the template and was the best, if not the only, friend I have ever had. I speak now of *true* friendship, and I suppose that means someone who genuinely enjoys your company and, above all, takes a sincere but un-intrusive interest in your thinking and your doings, and even delights in your achievements and worries about your wellbeing, unafraid to give sober advice if and when considered needful. A tall order? Yes, I think so. Yet not perhaps quite as tall as Saint Augustine's notion of a friend as 'one with whom one may dare to share the counsels of one's heart'. It may be very hard indeed to reveal the 'counsels' of your heart, even to yourself, even if they are known in the first place. Honesty in writing about yourself, for example, may be extremely painful, perhaps embarrassing, not to say shameful, and the vast majority of writers avoid it. But there is so much that is unknown about ourselves that the so-called 'Socratic' injunction 'Know Thyself' may be the hardest thing we are invited to do, as is 'To thy own self be true'. Most people are so ill-practised in being true to others that they have no idea how to go about being true to themselves, or they may have so little notion of what to be true about in themselves that their consequent inability to be true to themselves is mirrored in the expression of that inability elsewhere!

Suffice to say that John and I were undergraduates together at university college Swansea, he being a 'mature' student about 15 years my senior, reading German literature, while I read Philosophy. During this time he met Monika Wendle from Mannheim who was reading English. John and I were friends until his death. We ended up living far apart so that meeting face-to-face was a struggle. We both had, as people say, 'lives of our own to lead', but the long letters we wrote to each other were a continuation of the conversations we had as students together and which often lasted into the small hours. As well as being older than myself, physically he resembled my father. He took an interest in reading, was fond of classical guitar and taught me a few pieces, and he taught himself Latin so that he could read some classical literature in the original, believing that Latin and Greek were the most life-enriching languages we can become familiar with, as against the common view that, being 'dead' languages, they can have nothing to offer. He was quiet, reserved, thoughtful and considerate. He was a deeply spiritual man who had once come close to a cloistered vocation until he realised that he was not after all cut out for it – while at prayer he asked himself the question, 'What am I doing here?' Worldly thoughts intruded upon his prayers, and, he said, he knew he had to leave the cloisters. He was a man who clearly was not afraid to be honest with himself. His good wife died, and his own physical condition, already debilitating, deteriorated further as he struggled on hopelessly without her. I was informed of his death, and told that he had been found on his kitchen floor, cold and alone. And this image haunts me and will continue to do so until my own time comes. He was in his mid-to-late 80s when he died, but old age was not the sole contributor to his passing. He took a part of me with him when he shook off this mortal coil – well, some might say, that's how it is when people close to us leave us and parts of us are chipped away, and when it happens often enough it's a wonder that any part of us is left able to stand, for we become mere vessels full of bittersweet memories and unfulfilled wishes. But such a view forgets how much these people give us and make us what we are, hopefully far better than we would otherwise have been, which is why we owe an immeasurable debt to those we have loved, and continue to love even in death.

'What do you think? Should I?' he asked when as students we were out strolling one day. He was not really consulting me but thinking out loud and wondering whether he should marry Monika. I suppose I mentioned the usual commonplaces and platitudes: He was the only one who could decide the matter; Man was not meant to live alone; Companionship is important; If you really love her; etc. But I am confident that I didn't mention what the price of a partnership in love must entail – the inevitable loss and consequent unspeakable grief that death brings in its train. The greater and deeper love is, the greater and deeper the grief. At that time it hadn't really occurred to me and in any case would have seemed inappropriate. He married Monika and had several very happy decades together.

I was told that he took Monika's passing very hard. I believe he found it unbearable. He could not turn to alcohol. He had been a teetotaller all his life and believed drugs of any sort to be sinful. His only source of comfort was his unfailing belief in a Christian and loving God. I presume that even this was insufficient. He died of a broken heart.

It might be fairly said that I found him a substitute for my own father. I don't disagree. All I know is that he was a man in a million, and that my father would have taken to him himself. I was lucky to have met him. I have never met his like since, nor do I expect to do so.

An endearing and lasting impression of him concerns his unfailing professorial curiosity in things which most people, including myself, take very much for granted. Crossing a field one day on one of our walks and remarking to each other on a book he had read and had passed on to me, he suddenly stopped, stooped down and pointed to a clump of grass which to me looked like any other clump of grass and was therefore quite unremarkable. 'Well! Look at this! You rarely find this species in places like this. You see, it's quite different from the rest, if you look carefully. Amazing!' He said something about the colour and the shape and the texture – most of it lost on me. After pondering the matter for a minute or two we continued our walk, with me wondering what all the fuss had been about. He took a similar interest in birds and in trees, and he gave me a book on each of these subjects as occasional presents. He was ecstatic when Monika bought him a copy of *The Book of Kells* as a birthday present, and this, together with a work by Thomas Aquinas, prompted him to learn medieval Latin. I was reading philosophy and this endeared me to him. He had a deep respect from the Greek philosophers in particular and preferred Plato to Aristotle. Had he been able to fit it in. He might have learned ancient Greek as well to read Plato in the original. He was interested to hear what I had learned in lectures and loved to debate matters which he thought relevant to his own thoughts at the time. His curiosity was also inward-looking in that he believed that we as individuals should be subjects of our own investigations. I remember him speaking in this vein, 'We criticise others freely, but we should stop to examine ourselves more closely than we do. I often wonder why I feel in a certain way about something – when I feel upset or angry, I mean. Or I wonder why I said something the way I did, and whether it has upset someone and should have been left unsaid, or left un-thought, or unfelt. Yes, I think we should take ourselves to task more often.' He considered philosophy to be a tool of analysis and criticism or appraisal. He once said that philosophy is the handmaiden of theology and was mildly put out when I preferred philosophy to stand alone on its own two legs.

A man is rare who possesses rare qualities. It's little wonder that I shall not expect to meet someone of his ilk again. But these qualities must be respected mutually if we are to speak of friendship. John's personality and character were akin to my father's, or close to the template which I had inherited from him and used, consciously or otherwise, to develop a kind of mindset towards other people.

Before passing on, however, it would be remiss of me to fail to mention a person I once met in my student days whose name I never learned, a man I simply refer to as The Gardener – an extraordinary person encountered in commonplace circumstances who is not far removed from the template my father created and whom I therefore consider most worthy of note.

On graduating, John and I went our separate ways: he left for Mannheim with Monika and married her there. I continued as a postgraduate at Cambridge, feeling a little lost without him and Monika, especially in the evenings. It was on one of those evenings that I met The Gardener. I strolled out of the university precincts and found myself ordering a beer in a pub that was a little crowded. I found myself sitting at a small table in a corner of the room, next to a man in his mid-50s, clean-shaven, blue eyes and wearing a tweed jacket that had seen much better days. We exchanged glances and the customary form of casual greetings and, between sips of beer, he inquired whether I was a student and what I was studying. His accent was neutral and hard to place, but neither sophisticated nor distinctive in any way. I discovered he was a gardener in one of the Cambridge colleges, I forget which. His face lit up at the mention of philosophy and he proceeded to talk about one philosopher after another, including the Greeks. He seemed well informed, comparing philosophy with gardening and suggesting that the cultivation of an inquiring mind is akin to that of plants. He said something about nourishment and about neglect, something about the consequences of neglecting a garden and the neglect of analytical thinking and critical analysis. I was dumbfounded that he knew so much and was so adept at forming his own opinions and expressing them with insightful analogy.

The acquaintance was short-lived. 'Would you do me a kindness?' he asked, as he was about to leave. 'Could you write a few lines to say that I'm not a bad fellow?' I think I nodded with a quizzical smile. But he quickly changed his mind. 'No, no, never mind,' he said. 'But just remember that in this world the more good you try to do the more bad you will meet.' And with that he left and I never saw him again. I stayed for a while, sipping my beer and smoking my pipe (for in those more halcyon days pipes were permitted), trying to get my head round an experience I was destined never to forget.

I have often wondered what happened to him subsequently and why he had asked me such a favour. What on earth had he done? What had he been accused of? Such a simple, decent, intelligent man, and perhaps wiser than many who strutted around the halls of academe. It was just the kind of experience I would have enjoyed relating to my father, the question 'What would *he* have made of it?' nibbling away at the back of my mind.

Whether I had judged his character rightly or wrongly I couldn't, and can never now, say. But I do know where that judgement came from. I am deeply familiar with the template on which that judgement and every judgement I make about people is grounded.

It's astonishing how, in the most unexpected places and at the most unexpected times, such as a long, empty, dreary evening in Cambridge in an equally forgettable pub, an equally memorable event can take place.

Incidentally, on another equally dreary evening, John and Monika suddenly turned up on one such evening at my room in St John's and invited me to share a holiday on the Isle of Skye. I was quick to accept and was temporarily rescued from boredom. We spent two weeks on the island in an old rustic cottage and took long walks along the coastline, while in the evening we played classical guitar pieces and took time over our food. It was good to be together again. Walking with John was like walking with a vicarious father. Then we parted again, they returned to Mannheim and I was left with some fond memories. The Isle of Skye is not for those who derive pleasure and sustenance from the bright lights, for they say there that 'even the sheeps are lonely'. After Skye, Cambridge evenings seemed almost metropolitan.

11

RIPPLES IN THE WATER

A flat pebble skims on the surface of the water and ripples fan out like the consequences of a loss. I've already mentioned how I came to destroy the photographs of my father because my mother sobbed over them. Their destruction was not of course a cure, and much later we both came to regret bitterly what I had done. The road to Hell is paved with good intentions, and with the destruction of photographs. No cure, and my mother continued to feel his loss deeply, as did I. Christmases, as I have said, were a torture, for, try as we might, we could not suppress memory and the grief it engendered. My mother did her best. She would decorate the living room with seasonal trimmings and bedeck a small, simple artificial tree with candles and tinsel, and all was well for a few days, and then one by one, piece by piece, the trimmings would be boxed until hardly anything remained that reminded us that it was Christmas, a time of festivity. She had decorated the living room for my sake, but could not keep up the pretence. This process was repeated every year, with the regularity of a religious ritual, until, in her 80s, she succumbed to dementia and the whole idea of Christmas went the way of all rational conceptions – it became a blank and in doing so released her from the pain of recollection and repetition.

So much for the downside. Through the pain of grief and loneliness she became stronger and eventually more independent of spirit and of mind. My father had left us no money through no fault of his own, not even a generous insurance handout, just enough to cover the expenses of cremation and everything that goes with it. My mother became straight talking and strong minded. She was not a harridan, but if something upset her or irritated her it would need to come out, please or offend. She could show great tenderness and consideration for others, qualities which were rooted in great sensitivity and understanding. Through a simple lack of money, she was obliged to be parsimonious, and, allegedly like Elizabeth II, turned on an electric light on a quid pro quo basis: one light on, another light off. She would not tolerate wastage or carelessness when it came to expenditure and looked after every penny – not out of choice or meanness but of necessity, for I was a schoolboy and then a student and my vacation jobs were few and far between and hardly very remunerative. We lived simply together. She made some friends, though she would not call them that. She preferred the word 'acquaintances' or 'associates'. But there was one real friend, and his kindness towards myself and my mother was as selfless as might be expected in any human being, and she would not hesitate to call him friend, and nor would I. My father was for her, as much as for myself, a template in her relationships. Although he was far less sociable than she, his qualities seemed to become more apparent to her as time passed and she seemed to miss him as much in later life as she did in the beginning. In short, it might be true to say that my father's demise finally made a woman of her – though we would most certainly have wished to achieve that end with him, not without him.

It must be right that beautiful people should become memorable and inescapable templates. If my mother had been too young of spirit when she first married my father, as the years passed she came to appreciate his more sober disposition and calmer mood. It is as though she became closer to him than she had been when he was alive and consequently understood him better. It takes time for some marriages to achieve their spiritual consummation, like two lines which, at first divergent, finally meet.

The ripples that fan out over the lake also and obviously encompassed me too. The night my father died my mother and I swore never to part. She could read my thoughts and I hers, as though an invisible thread joined us together, but that thread was no more than the painful and shared recollection of someone deceased and wrongfully missing in our lives. A glance between us at Christmas, for instance, would seal the fate of merriment, for festivities would seem an impertinent intrusion on our grief. In this we did each other no good, and it was hard to keep things together sufficiently to prevent others participating in an aura of gloom – largely managed, but only just.

Such, then, was the depth of irretrievable loss and the sheer weight of memory – of a kind hardly unique to my mother and I, but perhaps less well survived than by many. It is 63 years since my father's passing, but that dark, cold night when the air seemed suddenly cold and still and time itself stood to attention is as clear as ever it was.

If templates and role models can exercise this much influence over the lives of others for the good, we must concede that there are also templates which can with equal or even greater force work their magic for the worse. Memories of my father, visually encapsulated in his portrait, are not I should say obsessive, certainly not fanatical. Yet the fanaticism and obsession almost invariably concomitant with political ideologies and systems of religious belief, and the mindless subservience that attends them, are responsible for much harm. Systems of belief that profess much and promise more but cause human catastrophe are frequently bolstered by portraits of their proponents, as though the mere two-dimensional representations of such leaders give sustenance to those that blindly follow them. How important then to link the good to the correct portraits and the right portraits to the good!

All of which is simply another way of saying that we should strive to create and promote the right kind of role models before we aspire to follow them, emulate them or allow them to inspire us, a wish reminiscent of Plato's injunction that we should pray to have the right desires before we pray that our desires are fulfilled. But I rather fancy that this, like so many prayers spoken out loud, is more a cry for help or a sigh of lingering despair than an expression of hope – or, at best, more an expression of hope than a serious expectation.

If I have praised my father in his capacity as role model, it is only fair to question my natural prejudices in his favour and ask, more 'objectively', whether he possessed imperfections as well as virtues. Since I was never, and now can never, be privy to the 'inner man', my answer can only have face value and must vie with the fact that the health of a tree must be measured by its fruit, the fruit being what I actually saw him do and what I heard him say and my impressions of his general conduct.

Amongst his imperfections are peccadilloes of taste and habit. Undoubtedly he smoked too many cigarettes and of the wrong kind, but this is not a weakness of soul but of habit. And perhaps he was overzealous in his distaste for alcohol as is exemplified in his judgement that pubs and clubs are 'dens of iniquity'. I can't help feeling that this phrase was lifted from his own father's text, for I am told that my paternal grandfather was a fire and brimstone lay preacher who brooked no departure from a 'pure' code of personal conduct. You may surmise from my use of inverted commas that I have difficulty supporting any view in terms of purity, since this is a concept which is as slippery as an eel and which may mean very different things to many different, but equally decent, people. One incident, if true, stands out. Apparently, one Christmas my father decided to visit one of his sisters. In jocular mood he knocked at the door and upon opening it she judged that he must have been drinking. Accused of insobriety, my father lost his temper and with it his jocular spirit. I am told he never lived it down and found it hard to forgive her error of judgement. We may fairly say, therefore, that he was apt to take a certain kind of joke far too seriously if, as I say, the story is true – and, if untrue, it nevertheless gives us a little insight into the conscience of the 'inner man'. I prefer to think that there is some truth in the story but that my father was no zealot for abstinence and found the whole episode laughable. However, it can be fairly assumed that he was teetotal, with no fondness for pubs and clubs, and no secret drinking!

Is any of this at all relevant to the man in the portrait and consequently to the portrait? I think not. No man can claim perfection, if only because the claim makes little no sense, nor, therefore, can it be claimed by one man of another. What then can be claimed? What is the very best that can be claimed, short, perhaps well short, of perfection? Good intentions. Though it is well documented that the road to Hell is paved with them, they can at least be said to emanate from a good heart, and a good heart is a loving heart. A loving heart is the best that can be expected from a parent. It is also all that can be expected from a child.

But a heart that loves is also a heart that suffers, which is why the ripples of loss never cease, for they never run their course but return to haunt those who grieve, like a flat pebble constantly returning to be thrown yet again and again without ceasing, without reprieve, without respite.

12

AND IF THE PORTRAIT SEES...

The portrait listens and even moves, but does it really speak? And if it sees, what does it say about what it sees? Famous portraits of leaders past may well invite speculations as to what they might say were they to see and speak now long after their time. Would Cromwell still bid the Commons to be gone since they have sat too long? And as he glances round the globe at the unspeakable inhumanities practised there, all in the name of some loveless god or monstrous dictator or some worthless piece of land, would he not find greater cause than ever to beseech people 'in the bowels of Christ' to think it possible they may be mistaken? Would Churchill believe his 'sunny uplands' to have been achieved? Would he think them ever even achievable? What would Gandhi say of present day India, or, come to that present-day anywhere and present-day anything? Perhaps he would simply sigh and leave it at that. We answer such questions according to the values which prompted us to ask them in the first place – but this is no place for political, moral or philosophical debate.

It is worth noting that my father gave me a sense of history. As I recall, there was only one history book at home, a large tome whose title and author I was too young then to recall now. My father would pick it up and study the pages as though they were fragile documents of immense importance. He gave me an idea of the importance of history, which soon became a sense of the continuity of history, a feeling that, ironically, time is irrelevant, as though the sameness of everything is what really counts. It's almost as though I expect Cromwell to make a guest appearance in the House of Commons putting the case for the abolition of monarchy or lambasting the Commons for its incompetence and moribund continuance. Or as though I should not be surprised to find Julius Caesar interviewed on television and asked to justify his 'Veni, vidi, vici'.

So much for the giants of the past. What of the common man? What would my father make of me as he stares out his portrait not at the world but at the odd little old face which stares at him? I imagine the portrait as a two-way mirror. Would he recognise his small son in the face of an old man – that face that salutes him with a wink every time he passes, those lips that sum up the day's events with a 'Good day today, Dad!' or 'Well, that's that!' or 'Not so well today, I'm afraid, bad mood'. Perhaps he would count himself lucky that the face does not, or has not yet, given him a running commentary or a speech or two on the excesses and deficiencies of mankind. But what would he say about what he sees?

Would he see in me what I see in him? Would he be proud or perplexed by what he sees, pleased or disappointed? But these are questions I cannot answer with confidence, for I am too close to myself and not close enough to him. I can hardly preach objectivity in others if I cannot find it in myself. I can, however, hope that I have a loving heart, and that that would be sufficient in a child as it is in a parent – one loving heart meets another, now what more can we possibly hope for than that? And so I should hope that the portrait that sees would find in this stranger's face a reciprocity of love, a mutual understanding, therefore, that is ready to forgive the peccadilloes and favour the good intentions flow from a loving heart, while the defects and deficiencies are, if not overlooked, at least viewed with a sympathetic eye. A reciprocity of love? Well, what else should we call it?

The face he sees has changed much from the face of the eight-year-old who was perched uncomfortably on the crossbar of his bicycle for what seemed a long ride into another world – that was the day we went picking hazelnuts from the trees in a field at the side of a road. He helped me down from the crossbar and over a stile and we set to picking handfuls of hazelnuts. 'I used to come here when I was about your age,' I think he told me. The long ride back, with my small pockets full of hazelnuts, must have been just as unpleasant. That was one of the very few times that we spent together – when my face was smaller and younger and free of unwanted lines, the face that my father would remember as he looks out from the wooden frame of his portrait. But the face in the portrait is much younger than the face I remember, for it is the face of a young man as yet undefiled by the sights and sounds of war.

What would the young face in the frame make of the old face that looks, stares and acknowledges him several times a day and in such an affectionate, caring, I shall not say obsequious, manner? Would he interpret such strange behaviour as expressions of guilt?

Feelings of guilt, it must be said, also cause long-lasting, far-reaching ripples on the surface of the lake, even when the cause or causes, real or imagined and created in childhood have long passed and are perhaps only half-remembered.

How could I possibly have neglected my father's Bible? Why was it not boxed and preserved, a monument to the man and to his memory – no doubt the very thing he prized above all his meagre possessions? What happened to his chromatic harmonica, the very instrument that requires the breath of life to be played and that therefore touched his lips and those of no other? And what of his pipe, that simple thing that had given him some moments of pleasure in a world he had learned to view with much circumspection and no small degree of naked astonishment at the inhumanities practised there.

Guilt is the arch enemy of mental stability – and indisputable evidence that when people are not warring against each other they are warring within themselves. One of the most vexing of questions is how to make amends to those who are dead? How is it possible to receive forgiveness from the dead, who are incapable of giving it, incapable even of hearing the lamentations of the living for their perceived failings? Lessons may indeed be learned, but how are they to be followed up?

Guilt is like a thorn in the flesh – painful, certainly, but to the good it is a pain that they would not exchange for any pleasure. A feeling of guilt is like male circumcision or a hair shirt. But it is also a guiding star, a compass pointing true north, a moral reminder, an *aide-mémoire* should the pain begin to fade and we are in danger of losing our way yet again. I speak of pain, but guilt, properly conceived, is a guide in a confused and confusing world and here the line between pain and pleasure is unclear. Pain is not what the dead would want to bestow on their loved ones – but they would gladly offer a guiding hand were they able to do so. Does conscience make cowards of us all? But what *kind* of conscience? In a good heart conscience works a noble magic and can make heroes of us all or, at least, prevent us from becoming even less heroic than we are already.

What can I conclude from these seemingly half-baked and pretentious ramblings? But I hope they express more than a hollow piety. My sense of guilt has made me more aware of my own shortcomings and has been a constant goad towards being better than I am or at least not worse than I am, with a desire to make amends for things that cannot be amended. It may be granted that at least the desire is important even if it is one that cannot be met.

A case in point: one of the Christmas presents I received from my parents, initiated no doubt by my father, was a set of four encyclopaedias for children. In the years that followed after his death, they, like many other books, were given away. Regret eventually followed in their wake, a regret that in turn was swallowed up in the minutiae of daily life. I needed to learn to live with the fact that these books, like many others, were now irreplaceable. Until, that is, many years later, I spotted a similar set of encyclopaedias in a second-hand book store. I felt morally obliged to buy them, for it was as though I had been forgiven for parting with them and was now given the chance to rescue not the self-same books but identical ones which had suffered a similar fate by someone else's hands. I brought them home, dusted them and placed them carefully on my bookshelf where they stand to this day. They are reminders of my youthful folly and a kind of atonement for wrongdoing – as if to say, one was lost, but one was found. I imagine that my father would have been pleased, not of course with the books in themselves, but in the knowledge that I had associated them so clearly with the Christmas present of many years past and with the fact that that present had come to me by his own hand. I have the same reflective and pleasurable thoughts each time I glance at them on the bookshelf. As I pick one out and glance over the pages and the glossy pictures, memories of my earlier childhood and of my father rush back like a tidal wave. I have never asked the portrait what it thinks, but I believe the smile is a smile of approval.

The irresponsible loss of my father's Bible, however, is another matter, and I refuse to indulge myself with the luxury of forgiveness. And while the demise of his pocket watch may be overlooked, that of his Blue Book may not. I vaguely remember seeing the Blue Book only once or twice and glancing through the pages. There were jottings about this or that and perhaps a poem here or there – I must confess my memory is hazy. But whatever the book contained it would be a source of comfort to me now and in the years that followed my father's demise – something real and dependable, some real, unimagined, source of communication. The notes written there were penned during my father's wartime experience and would have been of especial interest for that reason alone. As it is, I must rely on my imagination and on my relatively scanty and unreliable knowledge to form an image of the inner man – I believe that in this I do not go far wrong, but nevertheless the Blue Book would have been a good compendium of evidence.

Yet we do have some written evidence of the 'inner' man. My father wrote two poems to my mother during his fight against the mighty Führer. They tell us something of the inner man, for surely Maugham was right to say that what a writer writes depends on the kind of creature he is. I might add that simply *wanting* to write at all also tells us something, and then *what* he wants to write tells us a lot more.

In the silence of a starlit night,

Walking 'neath the stately trees,

I heard a gentle whisper

Carried on the unseen breeze.

T'was the sweet, tender voice of a loved one

With a message to comfort my heart,

A message of longing and yearning,

And a promise never to part.

It is the old yet ever new story

Of man and woman in love,

Telling the world that they are partaking

Of God's gift from above.

How sweet is the unending story

Of two hearts beating as one,

United in peace and happiness,

The battle of life fought and won.

Such music of love

Chapter 12

In the still of the night

Is something I ne'er shall forget,

Through darkness and sorrow

To the joys of tomorrow,

Love's golden torch is burning bright.

It lightens life's bitter pathway,

And sheds its brilliance around,

Sorrows and trials are easy to bear

Where the light of love is found.

Such is the simple story

Of two hearts in unity,

Travelling along the path of life

From time to eternity.

In the second poem we hear more about the lady whose tender voice he hears.

My thoughts freely wander

To a dear friend of mine

So sweet and so gentle,

So upright and fine.

My heart aches with longing

And tears unshed,

For this lovely lady

I'm longing to wed.

And lost in the spell of her presence
I rest contentedly,
Enjoying sweet moments of happiness,
Of Peace and tranquillity.
Would that my lips could utter
The longings of an aching heart,
The anguish, despair and sadness
That they would then impart.

Undying love for you dear
Is the call from deep within,
Pure in its simplicity and truth,
And undefiled by sin.
O for the gift of expression
And the power to tell you all,
Of thoughts that have never been uttered
And the sound of love's own sweet call.

Dear lady I tell you sincerely
The thoughts of a tortured mind,
The yearnings of a despairing soul
For the lady so true and kind.
Now let me add in conclusion,
Leaving all in the hands of God,
The person of whom I am speaking
Is Bles't with the sweet name of "Maud".

If it is evidence of the 'inner' man we seek, it will hardly be relevant to talk of syntax and rhyme or the literary wisdom of having chosen this or that word or the use of capitals, or the archaic use of contractions. A debate about whether what we have here constitutes 'good' poetry would be an impertinence of the lowest order.

These poems give us abundant evidence of the 'inner' man. How many men now write love poems? How many men ever did? And what does the writing of love poems show? Above all, they show an enormous sensitivity. The kind of sensitivity, and perhaps even to a similar degree, as that shown by Pablo Casals who when interviewed spoke about the beauty of a flower, a plant, a tree, the symmetry of nature. It is hardly imaginable that Casals would intentionally, let alone wantonly, crush a flower underfoot. It is the sensitivity of an artist. Of a true poet! The poems my father wrote are instances of true poetry and show him to have been a man well worth knowing and worthy of the deepest respect.

Such sensitivity, however, comes at an enormous price. It's no wonder that he mentions sorrow and despair, sadness, anguish and a tortured mind, darkness, and 'life's bitter pathway'. And we must speak of differences. One soldier kills his enemy and boasts about it, another may walk away shrugging his shoulders, and another may carry with him a 'tortured mind' for the rest of his life and find no consolation in the sentiment that God will forgive him, for what is forgivable in the eyes of God may not be forgivable by men. War may be necessary, but what is necessary may not be right, and what is wrong in the eyes of a sensitive soul may not be forgivable. A sensitive man may take the lash to himself for the rest of his life. He will also see about him a continuance of man's inhumanity to man long after the war is fought, and each instance of cruelty in peacetime is like a thorn in the flesh – and he will wonder to what good wars are fought when those who fought them or suffered the terrible consequences of them live as though there are no lessons to be learned other than those of military tactics and strategies.

As for my father's references to God, it seemed natural to him to talk of 'God's gift from above' for the 'gifts' that come from below are at best mixed blessings and at worst calamitous, and he must have found it comforting to leave 'all in the hands God' in view of all the inhumanities that ensue from the hands of men. Here we find a young man appealing to God in the midst of warfare, profoundly fearful of outcomes and struggling to comprehend the doings and thoughts of his fellow men. When good men can find little consolation in this world, they appeal to another, and when human leadership is wanting, they appeal to the divine. What men can't sort out, God will put right, and if Jerusalem cannot be built here, it can be found elsewhere.

Whatever we might say about religions, theosophies and religious belief and metaphysics, the appeal to God is a very natural cry of pain, an expression of despair, hopelessness and disillusionment with the terrestrial state of affairs.

And such appeals and expressions emanate from sensitivity. An appeal to God is not an expectation that the skies will open for Heavenly cavalry to descend and save the day. It betokens 'a tortured mind' and 'a despairing soul – but how enlightening, how suggestive, to find it in one so young! It is reminiscent of Chesterton's talk of 'a virgin astonishment' at evil, wickedness and inhumanity. Hope lies here, for if such an astonishment were to become universal, man's inhumanity to man might cease. Or is this simply a pipe dream?

What would my father say in response to this scant and inadequate analysis? I must consult the portrait next time I pass it on the stairs. Will the smile be somewhat restrained this time? Or will I sense a warmth of approval? Will the man who once tried to teach me how to swim stare with knitted brows at the old man he can't make out? What movement will I detect? Yet, whatever the response, I can only continue and do my best to reach that inner man, as I am sure he would do the same to reach me. We may yet be a reflection of each other, here on 'life's bitter pathway'.

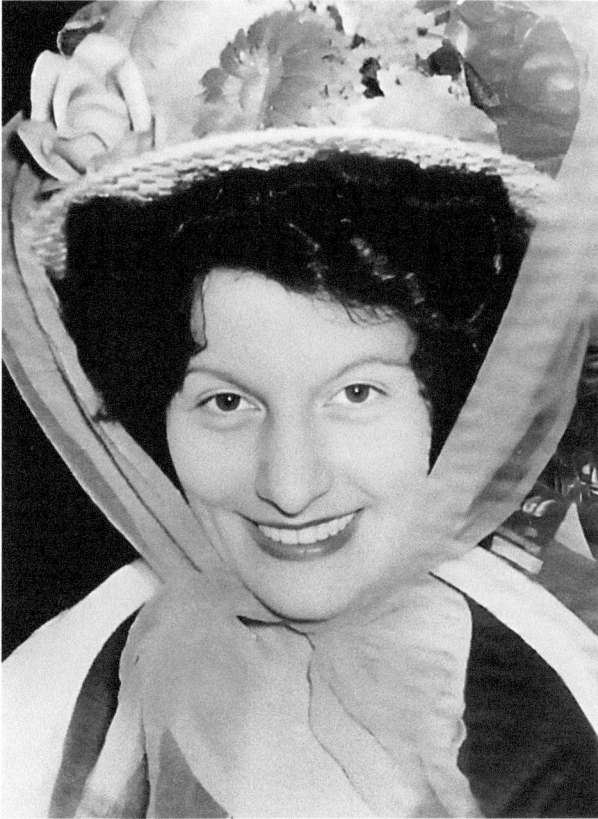
My mother, Dorothy Maud, in an Easter bonnet

13

LIFE'S BITTER PATHWAY

Much of the time the portrait is unsurprisingly noncommittal, but the smile remains. I allow myself some reasonable conjectures on its behalf.

And so I should say that 'life's bitter pathway' may be salved somewhat by friendship, good health and meaningful work. Faith in a loving God may seem to top the list for those fortunate enough to have preserved their belief in a world of shifting sands and human tragedy, though such a world may also strengthen their faith in a better one – for if there is no better, what is the point of it all? Very well. But what is such a faith and what is true friendship without love? Love must surely be the common denominator of all saving graces. Wealth and prestige are not to be counted, for they are easily lost and, when possessed, are apt to attract false friends and much envy and, worse, jealousy. Those with reputation and money are generally too busy preserving them to attract and enjoy the love of others, a love which they may well believe they can do without.

'Love' and its equivalent in other languages ought to be considered the most important word in the global lexicon, but not on account of the frequency of its use, for like an old hat worn by very different heads it has lost its shape. Most would agree that love is not to be confused with 'being in love', the latter being a transitory passion, the former a more permanent and reliable disposition to do good towards another. Falling in love may be instantaneous, but loving another needs cultivation and a chance to grow.

My father was 'in love' with my mother, and his poems are clearly an expression of that. But he also speaks of love as God's 'gift from above' and of 'leaving all in the hands of God'. He is speaking of the love between men and women, of personal relationships, and this should surely encompass more than simply 'being *in* love' and '*falling* in love', which are temporary states. It might interest us to know what the relationship is between God and love.

I have heard it said that 'God is love'. I would much prefer to understand this as a statement of conceptual equivalence, not of subject and predicate – but a universal concordance on this is very far from forthcoming.

Sexual desire and gratification is not to be confused with love in the statement 'God is love', any more than pleasure and its satisfaction is to be equated with happiness and spiritual fulfilment. An unhappy man may gorge himself on many pleasures, like King Midas, yet receive no sense of fulfilment, and a happy man may yet be sustained through the displeasures of pain – the sick man has his health up his sleeve, says Montaigne, and on his deathbed Wittgenstein claimed to have had a happy life, to the astonishment of those who knew, or thought they knew, him well. I shall take this as read, yet I cannot assert with absolute confidence that it would be so regarded universally, for there seems to be no end to disputation, even on matters that might appear relatively obvious – people are forever unpacking suitcases, even empty ones.

To engage in endless disputation is not my purpose here, but this I must say: that there are religions that are fond of employing the word 'love' though there are lamentably few instances of love to be found in them. Like the proverbial road to Hell, initial intentions may not always be sustained along 'life's bitter pathway', and the good that was meant can easily be forgotten in the webs that mankind weave and the jungles they cultivate, thinking them to be luscious gardens. The depth and breadth of human error is an ever burgeoning constant. But then, there are even religions that make no pretence of love whatsoever – their barrenness condemns them, for all they can offer is a extension of life in a 'paradise' filled with infinitely more of the pleasures their adherents have already had or the pleasures which they sought and were for want of wealth and opportunity denied. In religions such as these, what incentives could possibly be more hedonistic? Such religions entirely circumvent any discussion as to the logical properties of the proposition 'God is love' by making no place at all for it – indeed, instead, reference to God is proffered to justify all manner of inhumanities, deprivations, insanities and abominations. For such miscalled 'religions' as these, God is not love but death and destruction to all nonconformists, free thinkers and, above all, all those who are persuaded that love is the only God worthy of human submission – such a 'religion' is simply a political web of the very lowest kind, and their advocates no more than tyrannical politicians.

I look to the portrait for confirmation of this staccato of outbursts. The smile remains. However, once again, I cannot claim to know that the face in the portrait is smiling in agreement, or simply pleased that I should take an interest in such matters irrespective of whether what I claim to know and believe is in fact correct. Doubting what you believe is not necessarily a weakness. We know that it may be a spur to further self-reflection, but, much more than that, it is a rebuttal of the certainties that many claim to justify all kinds of tyranny, the kind of certainties that are no less than the very negation of love. For all his alleged faults, I hear Cromwell again, 'I beseech you in the bowels of Christ think it possible you may be mistaken.' The pity, of course, is that most people are uninterested in the 'bowels' of Christ but are firmly and irrevocably preoccupied with their own, suffering as they do from a form of intellectual and, *consequently*, moral constipation – if their thinking is wrong, so are their morals.

I can't remember my father ever discussing politics, though of course I was too young and otherwise engaged with playthings to register any such thing. But I vaguely remember his meetings with his brother, Ivor, who was a lay preacher, and an 'uncle John', when they would discuss aspects of the New Testament. But, as I think I can recall, these meetings, which took place in the living room of my father's house, were short-lived. My mother objected to the intrusion, possibly because too many biscuits and cups of tea were consumed without recompense of any form or to any degree. Money was in short supply and nothing was to be taken for granted. Quite right, too. But I suspect that she felt such meetings to be impositions that she was unable to deal with. They would have discussed matters which were entirely foreign to her interests. Such events would not have been considered 'social occasions'. Wives, who might have gossiped harmlessly in the kitchen, did not attend, probably for the same reason. She felt out of it, or so I imagine. So the meetings ceased, if only for the lack of a suitable venue.

Had my father given to Caesar what belongs to Caesar and discussed politics, it would no doubt have been about first principles rather than *party* politics. Fundamental moral values and how we should all endeavour to live our lives in the political arena or in any other, would no doubt have been discussed. There was little to say when principles were applied to political parties for it was generally taken as read that the Labour Party was the only genuine party of the 'working man', all others were for looking after Number One, and that therefore everyone had a moral obligation to vote Labour. This was the general consensus throughout the Welsh Valleys and an assumption so deep rooted that subsequent events have hardly dented it – and despite the fact that the lot of the 'working man' is in some fundamental respects just where it has always been and perhaps always will be. When Christ said 'The poor are always with you', he was not joking.

My father was, I feel bound to say, in the discussions and debates raging within himself, within the 'inner' man. His preoccupation, I hazard to guess, was how to square the many and persistent inhumanities mankind commits with the evidence, admittedly relatively sparse, of mankind's capacity for good – mankind's propensity towards evil with mankind's acknowledgement of love. After all, it was men who wrote the New Testament, as it is men who commit atrocities. To say that not all men are the same is a non-starter, for the problem is precisely how to account for the enormous gulf that separates them, and how, of course, to account for the equally disturbing differences that exist within every individual member of the human race, the capacity for wickedness that lies dormant even in those that wear the vestments of religious faith and which threatens to rise to the surface when their backs are turned, which is why the good pray not to be put to the test and why it is hard to trust even ourselves too far.

The good tend to be those who dare to think on such matters, and I am confident that my father was engaged in this inner turmoil, this never-ending search for some kind of acceptable explanation for the disparity between the good and the bad between men and in the heart of every man. I am tempted to say what is not quite correct, that the bad war against each other and the good war within themselves.

Naturally, I am merely speculating that my father was engaged in this inner turmoil. If I am right, it was his legacy and my inheritance, though I should claim to be a 'good' man because of it. Goodness is something one claims of others, but not of oneself, for fear of incurring the disdain of one's fellow human beings, for the number of generous critics is never legion, and here we can at least glimpse the dichotomies of the human heart.

If this kind of inner turmoil is my inheritance, is it a pain that I should not wish to exchange for any pleasure? I should like to say, doubt and uncertainty and the perplexity they engender maketh the man, certainty the automaton. But I do not say this out loud, merely in a whisper and in a darkened space. Of course, uncertainty and doubt must have just cause, and intellect, not intelligence alone, is required to perceive just cause. I speculate that my father found just cause for perplexity from his first-hand experience of war, and just cause for uncertainty and doubt as to the future of mankind – a doubting Thomas is not necessarily a fool, and not always someone to be ignored.

My father's experience of war would of course have been entirely unforgettable. The splinter of shrapnel lodged in his left hand, courtesy of the Vichy French, was no doubt an important *aide-mémoire*. The head of the splinter lay just below the surface of the skin, lodged there in perpetuity. I remember the head was bluish and was painful if pressed. Apparently, a medic had advised my father to leave it where it was since its removal would have been too problematic to make the procedure worthwhile. 'If it ain't broke, don't fix it' seems to have been the advice he received. The story fascinated me as a young child and has clearly remained with me.

(As an interesting side note concerning perplexity, uncertainty and doubt and the intellect required to perceive just cause, it is the business of philosophers to refuse to take for granted matters which everyone else assumes are beyond all reasonable doubt. For example, the question, 'Why should I be good?', which runs throughout the Socratic dialogues of Plato and continues in various forms to this day, is answered unquestioningly by many people with a simple, 'Because you'll suffer the fires of Hell if you're not'. Such 'answers' do not satisfy philosophers, because they also find just cause to question what such an answer could possibly *mean*! Similarly, language is generally taken very much for granted, but philosophers question what language *is*, how words can possibly *mean*, how *sense* is possible, how propositions can *say* what they say. Philosophers ask what logic is and how logic is *possible*. They are also interested to explore the concept of power, in politics and elsewhere. Philosophers are not fools for refusing to take such matters for granted – but if *this* statement were properly and universally understood, there would be many more philosophers and much fewer of their detractors, who either despise them or consider them simply eccentric and irrelevant. Philosophers find just cause to question the world in which they find themselves, not necessarily to change it but to *understand* it better. The source of their questioning has been said to be a sense of wonder. But we may add that philosophers may wonder at things which are not immediately explicable, like the nature of language and logic, or at the infinite varieties of chaos that humans make of their much vaunted 'civilisation'. Wonder and despair may well go hand in hand... But this side note is already too long, certainly long enough for any philosopher worth his salt to find just cause to question, alter and no doubt rebut.)

If my father's experience of war was an initial source of his 'inner turmoil' and abundant cause to speak of what he called 'life's bitter pathway', we must remember that fears which have their roots in the past are also projected into the future. Simply, what has happened before may happen again.

Near the portrait on the landing there is a window which looks beyond the garden and the playing fields in the near distance to a primary school. In the morning and during their playtimes, children can't be clearly seen from the window, but they can be heard. There are few sounds more comforting, joyous even, than the sounds of little children at play. Yet these same sounds are bittersweet, for any man with my father's sensitivities is bound to wonder about the kind of future these children will face. Even the sounds they make are often those of distress and discomfort, either real or imagined, for children love to imitate the sounds of battle and those of the killing fields of mankind – 'Bang, bang, you're dead' being a persistent favourite. Even in the playground you might speculate as to which of these children will turn out to be the man behind the gun and which in front. Children are delicate, vulnerable and impressionable, and there is, even from the earliest stages of their being, every reason to fear the influences and effects to which they are subject and are subjected. Hope and despair are mixed, and it may be the devil's job to separate them and give primacy to hope over despair. In the faces of little children one discerns the beauty of innocence, but a painful knowledge of what has gone before, generation after generation, might also fill you with a sense of foreboding.

Primo Levi's words sting like a thousand venomous wasps, 'Ci Sono individui particolarmente vigorosi, spietati, dishumani, con una Satanica cosciensa umana in cue la scintilla divina e' spenta per sempre.' He speaks here of people who are particularly vigorous and ruthless with a Satanical disposition in which the 'divine spark' is extinguished forever, an observation rooted in his experience of the concentration camp in which he was interred by the Nazis.

What worried Levi is that what has happened before might well happen again. The kind of people he describes above are, you might say, in the minority. Very well. But history shows that the minority is in the habit of becoming the majority. The rule of the mob is a persistent fact of 'human civilisation'.

What worried my father was what worried Primo Levi. Which is why the sound of little children playing is bittersweet. As Saint Augustine once remarked, 'The heart that knows acts like rust in the bones.' He who knows what dark things humans are capable of will suffer the pain of fear and foreboding. The 'inner turmoil' that I believe my father felt is due to the combat between hope and despair, and the overriding compulsion to make hope dominant in a world in which there is every encouragement to abandon it altogether. Yet again, John Bunyan comes to mind, 'Be ye watchful, and cast away fear; be sober, and hope to the end.' Not an easy thing for Bunyan, which is why he felt compelled to write about it in the first place, and in Bedford gaol at that! We ask: what does the future hold for our children? But also: what kind of future will our children create for themselves? What lies beyond the playground?

Is there anything that might sweeten 'life's bitter pathway'?

14

WORDS AND FACTS

Words like 'love' and 'God', which occur in my father's poems, are of especial interest to philosophers, or rather the concepts they denote.

I must confess I am not partial to sentimentality for its own sake, and so I have no wish to wring tears from the most vulnerable. Nor have I any wish to write anything that resembles a religious tract – I leave such things to the professors of their trade. There are those who use the word 'God' as though it were a stick to beat their opponents, and those who use the word 'love' to achieve morally dubious ends, and the differences between such people are often very much more apparent than real. I leave them to their unwholesome habits.

I am much more interested in facts, or what I perceive to be incontrovertible facts.

One such fact is that every human must die. Another is that the death of a loved one in particular is extremely painful, seemingly impossible, to bear. Another is that death may occur at any time, and this realisation is the ground of fear. Since it can occur at any time, and most unexpectedly, fear of death has been said to imply a fear of life, for every step taken may possibly be the last, and a life lived in a state of fear and anxiety is hardly worth living. Fear of loss and the grief it entails is an incontrovertible fact of life.

Are there mitigating factors that are equally incontrovertible facts?

Incontrovertible facts may take the form, or be transmuted into, platitudes. Platitudes are fated to become cliches, and cliches are boring, and things that are boring are apt to be ignored or taken with a grain of salt – like the familiar, such platitudes are treated with a degree of contempt and are considered instances of sheer sentimentality; they are placed on the back boiler of the human consciousness and simply forgotten. (In this, I am reminded of the contempt with which classical, so-called representational, art, or classical music, is treated by some moderns and in particular the younger generation. Bored by these exemplars of talent, it might seem intelligent as well as fashionable to look elsewhere for more modern, that is more 'advanced' or 'insightful' or 'imaginative' examples that push the boundaries of what is considered art or music. This urge forgets that what is different is not necessarily either more advanced or more insightful, but, on the contrary, retrograde. It is also a mistake to believe that classical 'representational' art is less imaginative than the abstract, for there is no such thing as art devoid of imagination.)

I look into the eyes of my father's portrait and I hear a platitude, or at least what my father would regard as an incontrovertible fact. I forget the precise occasion, but it is interesting that I recall him saying in conversation, 'Man wasn't meant to live alone,' and his adding, 'I could never live alone.' Did I hear him say this, or did my mother tell me that he said it? I can never know for certain. But the look he gives me in the portrait confirms that he said it, and the words have been in my head and associated with him since my teens.

So what's next? Do we simply overlook it as an expression of sentiment and move on as though it warrants no further consideration? I think not. If 'Man wasn't meant to live alone' is to many people too obvious for words, we should remind ourselves that the obvious is worth some reflection, like an old tune that is worth playing again.

Some images come to mind: it is sad to be alone in a sailboat on the high seas, whether or not the waters are calm. But when the waters are rough and storms come, two or more people can huddle together for comfort and hope. We may permit ourselves to think that those on the sinking *Titanic* at least found some comfort in one another before the very end, despite those who looked after themselves at the expense of others or those who put themselves first from start to finish.

For a teacher who enjoys his work, an empty classroom at the end of a lively and enjoyable term is a depressing thing. He remembers the interaction between and with his students, the jokes, the banter, the laughter, the questions and answers, the explanations that worked first time and those that didn't. He remembers the faces, now all gone, and not a sound breaks the air. He could almost wish the term was at its beginning again.

How upsetting it is to walk through the empty rooms of an empty house with memories of how busy it was with the sounds of conversation and laughter when your loved ones were alive, for all is emptiness when families are depleted one by one, and then there is nothing. A teacher might expect his students to return or for the old to be replaced by others. But when a family is depleted by death and nothing is left, there is no return. Ghosts are poor companions.

Consider a partnership, whether marital or professional. Two people are known as Jack and Jill. Mention of the one immediately brings to mind the other, so close and integral is the connexion between the two. When one dies, the sense of loss is profound, perhaps unbearable, for the other. Then, when both are gone, the empty space becomes the subject of much depressing thought and reflection, as though a whole world has been unaccountably swallowed up by some cosmic black hole. Jack and Jill went up the hill to fetch a pail of water (in other words, they lived and worked and thought and felt together), but Jack fell down and broke his crown (he died), and Jill came tumbling after (Jill died, too). When a professional partnership (say, a comedy act) is dissolved through death or ill health, the remaining partner feels an irreparable loss, and may well suffer a similar fate not long after.

These instances of togetherness are physical, in that they are examples of social interaction. When my father said 'Man wasn't meant to live alone' he was no doubt thinking of marriage. There is no doubt, I hope, that he would question the mere formality of marriage. He would want to speak of a marriage of *harmony*, not one which excludes love. Agreed, it is desirable to *like* the person you love if harmony is to be achieved, for it is possible to dislike the person you love. We might therefore say that love is a necessary but not sufficient condition of perfect harmony. In any case, 'love' is a word that is so difficult to do without, since it is a precondition of perfect harmony.

As the old song says, love and marriage go together like a horse and carriage, though we might add that not all horses are hitched to carriages, and that many carriages are quite horseless (cars, for example). My father was no doubt a devotee of marriage, because he believed that men and women should not go through life alone. (His views on same-sex marriage cannot be known and would not in any case

91

affect the general point that 'no man is an island unto himself'.) If love and marriage are meant to go together, it is hardly surprising that his poem seems to extol them as 'God's great gift from above'. No doubt he would say that without love there is no marriage, whether or not there is liking.

However, physical and social interaction is not all. Apart from marriage between couples, there is also 'marriage of minds' which need not, and often cannot possibly, involve physical or social interaction. And yet, a marriage of minds between people who have not met, will never meet, can never meet, is a balm which can ease what my father called 'life's bitter pathway'.

I think especially of literature and of how a book, or paragraph, a line or even a choice of word can strike a chord with the reader, such that a reader can find himself in what he reads and feels as though he might have written the words himself. It hardly matters much whether the chord struck is happy or sad. The important thing is that the chord is struck at all. 'Here is someone who thinks as I do' means that this reader is not alone. He has found a friend. It might be that what the writer says helps the reader to find a way forward in his thinking. 'I never thought about it in quite that way.' 'Yes, he has a point, perhaps it's like that.' Or perhaps the reader disagrees. 'No, that's not right!' 'He can't be serious!' No matter, for here the reader is communicating with the writer, and, if he reads on, the conversation may continue to his advantage, either because his own criticism is confirmed or because he comes to see that his reproaches are after all unfounded.

A reader finds that he is not alone even if he disagrees with the writer, because after all they are both on the same case! Disagreement may inflate the reader's ego, but now he has something to think about and someone to come back to should further reflection prompt him to reconsider.

This business of relating to the writer, being prompted by him, being spurred by him, is I believe one of the most important reasons for reading at all. It can be an important pathway of self-discovery. The reader discovers what the writer wants to say, but he also discovers something about himself. And isn't this what social interaction should be, discovery of others and discovery of oneself? The discovery of a marriage of minds is a comforting thing, and clearly something that is a mitigating factor on 'life's bitter pathway'.

Both reading and writing are means of self-discovery. A student says, 'But I've never thought about this, so it's hard for me to write anything.' This is not a reason for not writing but precisely a reason for doing so. He starts with a blank piece of paper and he thinks. Even if his first sentence is, 'I don't know what to say about this matter,' he might go on to give reasons, for the first line is like the first step of a journey, and in the process, arduous though it may be, he finds that he has opinions, and it often happens that these opinions change as he proceeds to write, so that what he says near the beginning is contradicted in his concluding paragraphs. Mind-boggling, mind-stretching, we test ourselves with a pen, and we truly do need to be tested.

But reading is self-discovery in concert with another, and if it happens that you meet a writer who travels the same pathway as yourself then you have made a friend. I have made many friends in this way. Charles Lamb, Bunyan (thanks to my father), J.B. Priestley, Boethius, Saint Augustine, Marcus Aurelius, Charles Dickens – no, the list seems endless. Yes, many of them are old, ancient and perhaps forgotten writers – for it so often happens that the classics are relegated to the fictional 'nursery' of mankind under the frightful illusion that new is better or best.

So when my father said that no man or woman should live alone, we might by extension talk of human interaction of all kinds, including the literary, even if our first thought is a physical togetherness in the same building or room. And this perhaps is the answer to the question of what can be done to ease 'life's bitter pathway'.

If this is a platitude, it is not a *mere* platitude, it is not one platitude amongst others, but deserves a very special place in our thinking and in our lamentably short list of consolations. No apology is given, for none is required.

Now, after all this rambling, I look again at the man in the portrait, and I glance again at a photograph of the woman he loved, and they both seem to smile in unison, united in death, as both my father and my mother would have wished. As for me, I doff my fedora (if I am wearing one), with a wink and a nod and continue the daily grind.

15

BEAUTY

'**B**eauty' is another word with a wide and somewhat treacherous currency. 'Now this is a beauty!' says the man, picking up an apple from the basket and holding it aloft. And what he means is simply that it is a very good example of its kind.

But I have no wish to talk about apples. The beauty of a poem is nearer the mark, and here we may return to my father's poems. An apple that is a very good example of its kind is not the sort of thing that is capable of moving us one way or another. It would be odd to speak of the 'power' of an apple despite the belief that one a day will keep the doctor away.

Simplicity of language and intention does not necessarily detract from the beauty of a poem. My father's poems have none of the complexity and obscurity of some of Dylan Thomas's, and they would not have had the ability to move my mother had they been equally inaccessible. Indeed, their virtue resides precisely in the fact that they are honest and open for all the world to see. They do not appeal so much to the intellect as to the heart, and therein, I should say, lies their beauty. When Lamb told Coleridge to 'cultivate simplicity, for there are no hot-beds in the gardens of Parnassus' he was appealing for openness, directness and an honest appreciation of what moves ordinary people, albeit here in matters of religious belief. I smile at my use of the word 'ordinary', as if to suggest that Coleridge was somewhat more than or other than human. But it is just true that people of extraordinary intellect, like Coleridge, can lose themselves in the byways and thickets of abstract reflection and find themselves far removed from the simplicity of thought and feeling that matters most to the rest of us – that very simplicity of thought and feeling that is capable of moving us deeply and that therefore matters most.

A simple act of kindness can move those who witness it to tears, as can the loving embrace of good friends. This is not to be confused with 'love at first sight', much less 'lust at first sight'. A loving embrace is devoid of passion and full of affection, for passion and affection are hopeless bedfellows. 'The world,' said Dostoyevsky, 'will be saved by beauty.' He was not here thinking of passion any more than the best exemplars of fruit. And when Plato said in his *Republic* (unapologetically I quote him entirely out of context) that the aim of education is to help us to love beauty, he was not thinking of young maidens in bikinis. For there is also a beauty in the logic of an argument, in which case we are no doubt referring to the 'power' of its premises to compel its conclusion. And from this we might conclude that beauty is a house of many mansions, in that it can take different forms and be of different kinds, just as the love of 'good' music is different from the love of a mother for her child, and the latter different from the love that a child feels for her pet kitten, and none of these comes near the love someone feels for their job. We might go on, but shall not.

My father's poems have the power to move precisely on account of their simplicity, their direct appeal to our emotions and their direct emanation from his own. Please note that by praising the humbler poets, I do not mean to denigrate the greater, but only to give the lesser their full due.

Charles Dickens is at his funniest when he caricatures characters and situations. He is at his most endearing and touching when he depicts simple acts of kindness and allows his characters to utter simple words of friendship and advice and love (devoid of the passion of lust). There are innumerable examples, too many to cite. But, in *David Copperfield* (Ch. 15), note the very touching contrast between the straight-talking and seemingly mercilessly harsh demeanour of Trot's aunt and her advice to him upon his departure:

'Never,' said my aunt, 'be mean in anything; never be false; never be cruel. Avoid these three vices, Trot, and I can always be hopeful of you.'

I promised, as well as I could, that I would not abuse her kindness or forget her admonition.

'The pony's at the door,' said my aunt, 'and I'm off! Stay here.'

With these words she embraced me hastily, and went out of the room, shutting the door after her. At first I was startled by so abrupt a departure, and almost feared I had displeased her; but when I looked into the street, and saw how dejectedly she got into the chaise, and drove away without looking up, I understood her better, and did not do her that injustice.

The beauty of simplicity bereft of sheer sentimentality is Dickens at his very best. My father was no Dickens and no Shakespeare, but his purity of heart is shown in the simplicity of diction and sincerity of feeling, elements that belong to the very best poetry, devoid of affectation and an overwhelming desire to impress with flamboyancy and strained elegance. Wherein, then, does true beauty lie, in the heart or in the eye?

The phrases 'a beautiful life' and 'a beautiful mind' are evidently expressions of approval, but it seems perverse to apply them to ruthless and cruel tyrants, to the selfish and the self-seeking, to murderers and torturers, or even to those who mass wealth for its own sake. The phrases are meant to praise lives of self-sacrifice or extraordinary tenderness towards others or to those who are resilient in the face of injustice towards themselves – resilience and the absence of desire for indiscriminate retribution. Mother Teresa's 'inner beauty' is a case in point, since her life was one of self-sacrifice and self-abnegation. Joseph Merrick's (the 'Elephant Man's') 'inner beauty' is his tenderness and his apparent refusal to blame others or the world at large for his misfortune. Self-sacrifice and 'purity of heart' seems to be what this kind of beauty is all about. The sensitivity of creative people or those who are exceptionally talented is also a candidate for such phrases as 'a beautiful mind', and here I think of Pablo Casals who was capable of shedding tears at the sight of a beautiful flower, so moved was he by symmetry and form. One would be hard put to imagine a man like Casals treading wantonly on flowers, even dead ones. Casals, the world's greatest cellist and a chief exponent of the works of Bach, was capable of moving people through the works of that great composer. It is not perhaps too ludicrous to say that the symmetry he found in Bach was reflected by what he saw in nature and the world of plants and trees. He was a man of obvious and profound sensitivity. How many men cry at the sight of a flower, or stare for hours at trees as though in silent communion with them? Poets do, and few would deny their sensitivity, while at the same time wishing they would 'pull themselves together, get a life and contribute something more relevant to the practicalities of life!'

We seem to have come a long way from a consideration of the simplicity of my father's poems. But perhaps just a side street or two, for I remember Casals himself saying that his life was simple, that he preferred to live a simple life. Have we said enough about beauty and simplicity? Certainly not. We have not even begun to scratch the surface if we wish to produce a philosophical analysis worthy of the name. But then, I have no wish to produce such a thing, which would require another volume or two and be of such a kind that even the most fearless of readers might find overly daunting, for there is nothing simple about simplicity when philosophers get their hands on the concept. Thankfully, it is not at all necessary to pursue the matter further. Suffice to say that the world could do with a great deal more of the beauty and simplicity of which we have been speaking.

Would my father agree with all or at least most of this? I believe he would, for his acquiescence would seem to follow from the very nature of his two poems, and from the bare fact that he wished to write them at all to the sound of artillery. Talk of beauty and the simplicity of a pure heart seems most appropriate now that Christmas is again upon us, a time when the contrast between how people should live and how they do live is most stark. Someone has observed that virtue is boring and vice is interesting, so that the incentive for the former is significantly weaker than for the latter. This too seems to be an incontrovertible fact of life. What is incontrovertible is inescapable, and so we are stuck with it. No doubt my father would agree with that, too. I am reluctant to look at the portrait, for fear that the expression has altered into something rather solemn and forlorn.

In spite of everything, the smile's disappearance is only temporary. It will return – doubts and uncertainties fully accounted for.

A few remarks are in order, however, touching the matter of hope. When Dostoyevsky said, or caused one of his characters to say, that the world will be saved by beauty, was this an expression of hope? Or are we to take him as saying something like, 'If the world is ever saved, and I'm not saying it ever will be, then beauty is the only thing that could ever possibly save it'? In other words, is the statement 'The world will be saved by beauty' a simple prediction, or is it a grudging expression of hope?

If someone hopes for good weather so that the clothes might dry on the line, the hope is reasonable if there is evidence to support it. If someone hopes that he will achieve promotion, he is assuming that a number of factors will combine to make it possible: that a position is or will be available, that his work will be appreciated, that he will be noticed, that he is next in line, that his face fits, that his health will permit it and… well, that no other factors will stand in his way. The validity of his hope for promotion is conditional upon a variety of factors both foreseen and unforeseeable – in other words, his hope is *grounded* in such factors if it is to be reasonable. My hopes to become the pilot of a jumbo jet, or a light aircraft for that matter, are undoubtedly ungrounded and therefore unreasonable for reasons of age and poor eyesight amongst other things.

My father's poems are themselves expressions of hope in that he probably would not have written them if he had thought it certain that they could never be read or certain that he could never survive the war. He hoped they would be read, above all by my mother, and that he would survive the war. Note the lines in the first poem:

Through darkness and sorrow

To the joys of tomorrow,

Love's golden torch is burning bright.

And we must remember that, in the second poem, he is 'Leaving all in the hands of God'.

He has hopes for the 'joys of tomorrow' and that all will be taken care of by divine intervention.

Hopes for the 'joys of tomorrow' are not at all irrational. He clings to possibilities, but they are *real* possibilities, even though they are conditional upon military outcomes. Military outcomes *can* ensure victory, and victory is the fundamental condition of 'the joys of tomorrow'.

But the idea that the world will be saved by beauty seems to be taking a very broad sweep, as though it were suggesting that 'human nature' can change for the better and produce a kind of utopian future for mankind, putting an end to man's inhumanity to man and ensuring a universal state of universal love. Is this a fair understanding of 'the world will be saved by beauty'? I can't say, and Dostoyevsky isn't around to clarify matters, either. I rather believe that he would take issue with the character who mouths this statement, but I can say no more on this.

But is the hope that human nature will universally change for the better a reasonable hope? I hardly think so. If it were possible, human beings would cease to be human, and such a state is very probably not one to be welcomed.

However, the plain truth of the matter is that human beings go on with or without such a hope, and the question of whether it is a reasonable hope never arises, except perhaps for philosophers. Entertaining such a hope changes nothing, not even a jot. You say, 'We can't go on like this.' Yes, but that is precisely how we do go on. Just as we say 'I can't go on like this' and then proceed to go on just like that. Life, the world, can't go on like this! But this is how it does go on. In this mess of a state, we pick out the best things and praise them, and we point to what is bad and deplore it. For consolation, we enjoy bits and pieces – a good meal when hungry, a pleasant drink when thirsty, friendship, good company, satisfying work or hobbies, having children and watching them grow up to be decent.

In short, we are stuck with what we are, with what we judge others to be, and with what we have and with what we do not have. Will the world be saved by beauty? Perhaps this is the wrong question. Perhaps the question should be: will human beings allow the world to be saved by beauty? Beauty is fragile. Many things that are thought beautiful now may not exist in one, two, three hundred years, and therefore will be incapable of appreciation. Vital forms of beauty, including that which we see in nature, may cease to exist, and they may do so at the hands of human beings, for this is what human beings do. In fact, it is what they do best. Human beings are imperfect, and therefore, one is tempted to conclude, everything they do, say, produce or construct is imperfect. Everything is imperfect, one screams, except the mess they make of the Earth and the perfect mess they make of human lives. And this is a fact that we are stuck with. If imperfection is all we have and all we can expect, life must consist of making the best out of a bad job, making the best of the little good that humans do, reproaching them for what they do imperfectly, striving against the bad that they do, and, concerning the things that cannot be changed for the better, tolerating as far as humanely possible what cannot be changed, namely all that which is uncomfortably squeezed under the umbrella of 'the human condition'. Unfortunately, the good that humans do is apt to weaken in its effect, and, like a piece of crumbling classical architecture, fade into the background, its place taken by what humans call 'unstoppable progress' and 'positive change', forgetting that few changes are changes for the better. The beauty of nature, of poetry, of literature, of music and of art are all fragile, just as even simple good manners and social etiquette may soon be eroded by habitual selfishness and thoughtless slavery to the routines of everyday life – it is only necessary to observe the behaviour of commuters on the subway to put blind optimism in its place. Bad habits are notoriously hard to break, and without sufficient corrective examples, may become unbreakable and therefore irreversible.

To say that nothing humans do is perfect, that perfection is a myth, is open to the accusation of negativity and cynicism and therefore of being a lopsided view. But man's inhumanity to man cannot be rubbed out by works of art, nor can they be righted by 'good works'.

My father's hope was that, in the war in which he found himself, good would triumph over evil, freedom over oppression – but a triumph and a freedom that would be limited and temporary. Nothing universal was guaranteed, the victory he hoped for was not one that could have application in all places and at all times, no utopia, no paradise on Earth, no end to all wars. After all that unspeakable loss of life, Plato's terrible and ominous words still rang true, as they ring true today and for ever more, namely that only the dead have seen the end of war. But that strong desire for a universal and eternal end to all wars is of course an expression of anguish, akin to a cry for help, a distress call in an empty wilderness full of lessons unlearned and all the recalcitrant and unheeding pupils that make up what is called humanity. Nothing learned, nothing gained.

At least some of my father's hopes were realised. My mother received the poems and treasured them all her life long, and he lived to see his 'joys of tomorrow', for he had a tomorrow to enjoy, thanks to people like him and to all those who 'gave their today'.

He did not know that *his* tomorrow would be short-lived, that he would not see his son marry and have children. There is much about such things that he would never live to know. But concerning other matters, not so. For this at least can be said, that my father, like many others, came into the world knowing nothing and left it knowing too much.

Did the face in the portrait wink, or did I imagine it? This much is true, that whatever I see in the portrait, whatever I hear it speak is seen and is heard by me and by me alone. For its power, whatever it is capable of giving, comes from me and no one else. When it speaks to me, I give it its lexis. Only the poems give word to the soul of the man, and all I can do is give it some space, as though I supply the thread that joins the needle to the fabric. Therefore, after me, when I am gone and soon forgotten, the portrait will hang mute and still, just a face amongst all others, a face in a sea of faces, no better or worse than any other. What then of the beauty of the portrait? Or should I say the beauty *in* the portrait. Of course, if beauty is simply in the eyes of the beholder, and if the beholder can no longer see, but has only the dead eyes of a corpse, we must presume that the beauty in the portrait dies also. Or is that too presumptuous?

16

THE ONE DAY

What did my father's demise take away from my mother and I, and what did it give? Such a question seems out of place and insufferably selfish and self-centred, ignoring entirely the fact that it took everything away from my father himself, for that of course is what death does – it takes everything away, all that man has, so that if no one exists to remember him, he becomes nothing, not even a memory. The question resembles the heading to a balance sheet, as though his death was some sort of transaction that can be weighed in terms of pluses and minuses. The infinitely greater loss, therefore, was suffered by my father. The incomprehensible, perhaps 'unimaginable' is a better word, absence of one's own very being, is a guarantee that in one's own death there is no sensation at all either of pleasure or of pain. Nothingness is impossible to imagine, but is no less real for that.

But, and as we all know, those who are left to mourn the loss of loved ones cannot be left out of account. For they, still in the land of the living, are more than capable of the sensation of pain, the pain of loss, of grief, of regret if not of remorse, of loneliness if not of abandonment.

Christmas time, and in particular Christmas Day, is the one day of the year in which people who should be together more often can be united. Perhaps the jokes about family rows on Christmas Day base their validity on the fact that people aren't together enough rather than the other way round. Peace, unity – well, too much may be made of them, but the least we can say is that Christmas Day is the one day of the year

102

in which efforts should be made to embrace the fellowship of loved ones, even if, often through trying too hard, we fail to take full and proper advantage of the occasion. Around the dining table toasts may be offered up to dearly departed friends and loved ones, and then, the toasts forgotten, the enjoyment begins or resumes – yes, but this was never enough for my mother and me.

It may be said, without exaggeration or rancour, that my father's death robbed us of Christmas. In all the many years that followed, and despite our very best efforts, Christmas, even the very mention of the word, acted as a trigger for a depression of spirits that reached its peak on Christmas morning and lasted until midnight that day. I said 'despite our very best efforts' because efforts were indeed made – presents were planned, bought and wrapped, cards were written and sent, and there were smiles and hugs all round, while compliments were made to all those who had made great efforts to provide the best meal we'd eaten all year. But behind all this was the ghost of my father, the horror of his untimely demise, and the sense of loss, as deep on Christmas Day as on that very first Christmas all those years, all those decades, ago. Santa Claus lost his magic and perished with my father, and Christmas and Christmas Day hobbled along on crutches for the rest of our lives.

There is no doubt that my father, like all those who love and are loved in return, must have worried about those he would leave behind in the event of his passing. For us all, there are at least two preoccupations: the fear of dying, the fear of how our loved ones will cope without us in a world such as this. The fear of dying is no doubt as rational as the fear of pain. But our fear about how loved ones would cope without us has something of the irrational about it, since the worst we can imagine for them would hardly be avoided if we were alive and well – indeed, our presence would often contribute to their predicament, through our own incompetence or by our becoming an extra source of worry. Nevertheless, the love we feel for them ensures that we shall worry about their fate. But since their ultimate fate is something that they, like everyone else, must face, it is perhaps a blessing that parents, for example, should die before their children and therefore be spared the unspeakable grief of losing them.

My father's passing also deprived me of his narrative and thoughts concerning his own life experiences, especially concerning the war, a vacuum that was filled by a gentleman whom we fondly referred to as Old Jack. Old Jack married my widowed grandmother and lived with her for ten years, a period of time he had himself predicted. 'If we have ten good years together,' he said, 'we'll have nothing to complain about.' They had been sweethearts in their youth, and now at last they could be together again.

But Old Jack's experiences concerned the first world war, by comparison with which, he said, the second world war was a picnic. He seemed to like nothing better than to curl up in his armchair by the fireside and narrate his experiences, punctuating his narratives by puffs from his Kapp and Peterson pipe which he kept lit with a taper which he ignited in the red hot coals of the fire. He hailed from Galway, and his Irish lilt was captivating, but a fascination with the stories he told saved me from somnolence. He had a lot to say, and he was grateful to have in me a very ready audience.

I respected Old Jack, and admired him. He had been awarded the Military Medal for outstanding bravery and his story concerning how he had come to earn it fascinated me. I do not think I can describe him as a mentor, but he did, as it were, stand in for my father, whose narratives had been stolen by death, and he did inspire me to take up pipe smoking, about which I have no regrets.

On the subject of mentors, during my years as an undergraduate and after reading Plato, the philosopher Socrates, became a kind of mentor, a kind of 'father figure' as it were – someone to whom I appealed for enlightenment and support, in much the same way that people appeal to God. Old Jack and Socrates had become, I suppose, courts of appeal in a world that seemed increasingly deficient in wisdom or, perhaps I should say in comfort. Old Jack's narratives about the horrors of war, and Plato's description of a man so despicably treated, did the job of educating me as to the shortcomings of human nature – and I rather fancy that they did the job too well, as did a reading of Robert Graves's *Goodbye to All That*, an account of life in the trenches which got a clear thumbs up from Old Jack for its accuracy and poignancy. My take on human nature would never be the same again – a quick, sharp series of shocks in my late teens from which I never managed to recover.

During all this time, and in fact only until comparatively recently, the portrait of my father, although kept safely and respected, was out of sight in the attic. A few years ago it was brought into the light of day and hung on the wall of the landing at the top of the stairs, as I have already described.

The portrait has come to form of the apex of an isosceles triangle, with Old Jack and Socrates at its base. How can it possibly be that the inert portrait of my father is now my chief mentor based solely on the scant memories I have of him?

Those memories, though scant, are accurate and powerful. They are, admittedly, no more than snapshots of the man that was my father, but I believe that snapshots can be as revealing, if not more so, than a studied portrait. Even so, it is on this flimsy basis that the portrait may be said to function as a mentor, though the words that I imagine emanating from his mouth are as much mine as the questions I ask or the remarks I make. It might therefore be said that I am no more than mentoring myself when the portrait 'speaks', and no more than listening to myself when the portrait 'listens'.

I might as well ask myself, 'What would he say?' or 'What would he do?', questions which we all ask of the dead, who cannot themselves speak and cannot themselves listen. Nothing new here. I remember that, as a student, I would ask similar questions of Socrates, even if, had he heard them, he would have been hard put to comprehend them, even in Greek. It is as though the dead, even those whom you never knew or could have known, become a second conscience, almost as the House of Lords is said to be a check on the ill-considered ambitions of the Lower House.

(Such communion with the dead is of course a function of how much you value them, whether or not your estimation of their worth is justifiable, for I have no doubt that there are those who enjoy silent communion with the despots, tyrants and mass executioners of the past on whom they lavish their praises and base their aspirations.)

The man in the portrait might then be said to live through me, as though he had been given a second and insentient life – if the phrase 'insentient life' is a contradiction in terms, it should be remembered that not every contradiction is meaningless. My father lives his insentient life as a member of the family, though no one else would call him a 'member' of anything. What matters is that he is *to me* a living ghost (another contradiction?), an airy after-image of the man that was, still capable of overseeing events, still responsive to the needs of those who place such faith in his advice and solicitude. And so the dead in their portraits still live, without taking one single breath, without taking one single step outside the frame in which they are encased. Ghosts they may be, but not of the variety to be shunned. If they are not truly our mentors, they at least enable us to mentor ourselves through them. They are, as it were, filters through which we may pass our feelings and ideas, enabling us to reconsider and advise *ourselves*.

This is what my father's passing gave me, the gift that was so mournfully wrapped and was hardly recognisable at the time. The gift was offered in exchange for Christmas Day. The myth of Santa Claus was replaced by the insentient image of my father in the portrait on the landing at the top of the stairs. The gift of filtering explains why any account of my father must also be an account of myself, why his 'biography' is my 'autobiography', if we are allowed to stretch these words to their limits, and why no one else is capable of writing it. My father becomes me, and I become my father. If so, we might ask what might become of me should the portrait be lost or destroyed – a question which may be unanswerable.

Were it possible to exchange that gift for the real thing, to bring back the life that was lost, would I do so? Would I exchange the portrait for my father of flesh and blood? Perhaps. But not without hesitation, not without deliberation, not without apprehension. Why?

17

THE LUCK OF LAZARUS

Lazarus of Bethany, we are told in the gospel of John, was restored to life four days after his death by Jesus, and this event ranks as one of the miracles performed by Christ. Granted that we have no trouble at all with concepts like 'miracle', 'perform', 'event', and 'restore to life', which is to grant a very great deal indeed, we must ask whether Lazarus thanked his lucky stars that Jesus was around to raise him from the dead. Other things being equal, which they need not have been, we can no doubt assume that Lazarus, and all those who loved him, rejoiced to see him alive and well again. However we should add that Lazarus was fortunate not simply to be restored to life, but that he was restored to life after only four days. True, much can happen in a short space of time, but little is expected to happen that would alter the very landscape, the very culture, and the very mindset and the very physiognomy of the people you know. It is reasonable to suppose that waking up after four days would leave you feeling that you have had a very long sleep – a little stiff in the joints and a little fuzzy-headed, perhaps, but happy to be surrounded by people and things familiar and wholesome.

But suppose Lazarus had been restored to life 40 years after his death, would it then be reasonable to suppose that everyone and everything would be just as it was when he died? Granted that within the politically, culturally and technologically limited parameters of the time, there would be much that he still recognised, but some of his nearest and dearest might well have passed on or have altered beyond recognition, and this might cause him some consternation to say the least. And are we to assume that after 40 years Lazarus looked just as he did when he died? If so, this may pose a few problems amongst his closest relations, for 40 years is a long time, and the discrepancy between ages may take quite a bit of getting used to. Or perhaps Lazarus is raised looking 40 years older than when he died, and this might cause additional stress for himself. Would he be recognised? Would he recognise himself? It is perhaps not too much to suppose that restoration to life after such a long time may cause much distress, disquietude, and psychological trauma to a degree that would defy straightforward readjustment. Far more than that which is required for a four-day absence of consciousness, namely a simple workout for muscles and joints and breathing exercises to clear the head.

We may now leave this idle, almost comic, piece of conjecturing, the sole purpose of which is to point out that a space of four days does not carry the implications of a period of four decades. We may add that raising Lazarus from the dead may be seen as an act of compassion as well as an index of the power of God or of Faith in that power, given, that is, that further life for him would not be an incurable living hell. But once the power to restore life is granted, it should hardly be a problem to ensure that the life restored is worth living. The act of restoring life must surely be as good as the act of preserving it when it is threatened, as good, in other words, as the sentiment upon which the Hippocratic Oath is founded.

By now, my father has been dead for more than 60 years, and it must be questioned whether restoring him to life after such a lapse of time would be as compassionate as it might seem to some – or seem to me, guided as I so often am by my emotions. I am not at all sure that it would be pleasing to have it pointed out to him that I am his son. For I am not the boy, barely in his teens, that he last saw. Nor would it be wholesome to tell him that the lady who was once the subject of his love poems grew old, developed the crippling disease of dementia and died divested of all dignity. Issues of physical appearance and the recognition or non-recognition of loved ones apart, it is highly questionable whether it would be compassionate to restore him to a world which for many reasons he could hardly recognise and which in some ways falls far short of the world he left behind.

Like Lazarus, my father might be restored to life, but deprived of the luck of having had only a four-day leave of absence. Unlike Lazarus, there would be little for him to enjoy. Instead, there would be much cause for sorrow, disappointment and disillusionment. Explaining this enables us to turn full circle in an assessment of my father's character, an assessment based on my scant memories of the man. The power of the portrait is the power of the man, and the power of the man is that of his character, and his character is shaped by his values. So what could I tell him were he to live again as the man I remember, as distinct from the young man in the portrait, after over six decades of nothingness? What could I, now an old man in a fedora, say to my father, in his 40s, that could smack of some kind of consolation for all those lost years? Consolation? On the contrary, he would be met with a litany of negatives.

It seems too obvious to speak of the persistence of war when Plato long ago said what by now seems patently obvious and profoundly tragic, namely that only the dead have seen the end of it. Nevertheless, my father's despair at being told that war is as persistent as ever, and that even the prospect of global nuclear war is not simply a theoretical construct, not simply a hypothesis we construct to amuse ourselves in contemplating the impossible, but a real possibility – his revulsion at this realisation would of course be predictable. He *might* have thought that the end of the second world war would see a universal reformation of character, a glimpse of a new and morally superior world order. I cannot claim to know what he *would* have thought, but I believe he was not acquainted with Plato, though he might well have agreed with the philosopher's gloomy announcement. His response, in any case, could only be, 'No change there, then.' He would be given ample evidence, since his demise, of tyranny and despotism, of dictatorship and submission, and shown too many instances of how and when the world has been, and continues to be, brought to the brink of destruction. He would see that world politics is governed by leaderships that collectively resemble a mafia consortium thinly disguised as democratic. In other words, the world to which he would be restored is decidedly no better than that which he had left. Cruelty, inhumanity, stark poverty, political deception and a predilection towards war still exist in abundance. Nothing learned, nothing gained. The poor, as Jesus is supposed to have said, may always be with us, but that is no recommendation for abject poverty, while *lebensraum* is no excuse for war, and the need for survival is no excuse for man's inhumanity to man. The temptation to conclude that everything that is attributable to the worst in human nature is both the cause and the effect of discontent and dissension continues to dog the thoughts of those who still have eyes to see and ears to hear.

So much for platitudes.

Though a spiritual man, he was not, as I think I have already said, a 'Bible puncher', a proselytiser, but he would be deeply saddened by the decline in church and chapel attendance and the near non-existence of Sunday Schools. Precisely because he was himself a spiritual man, he would have bitterly lamented the decline in a kind of self-searching and compassionate spirituality in others. It would not be the absence of ornamentation and ritual that he regretted, nor the blind following of doctrine or the uncritical acceptance of chunks of scripture, for none of this is 'spirituality' in what I feel bound to call the 'truer sense', any more than a church is where God may be found. Spirituality must involve self-examination and self-criticism as much as it does acceptance, which can be clearly seen in such unpopular, unread, because comparatively unknown, books as the *Confessions* of Augustine. But then of course, Augustine was a *saint* and therefore hardly stereotypical of the average man.

Next in the litany is communication. He would no doubt be impressed by the advent of the 'smart' television and the 'smart' phone, hardly believing that contact can be made in real time between people who can actually see and be seen – his reaction may be reminiscent of that of the Lakota Chief Sitting Bull's when he was first introduced to the telephone. Surely, this is not a negative but a resounding positive! But then it would need to be explained that despite the ease with which one person can communicate with another by means of the smart phone and messaging and texting and emails, people are as lazy in responding to them as they were when the only recourse was the letter and envelope. Moreover, the substance of what they have to say to one another over 'social media' is as crass as ever it was when they were separated by the garden wall. The general point here being that it is not simply technology and its advance that we must consider, but the development of technology in the hands of human beings. The motor car is a very fine thing, but human beings still manage to kill themselves and others by the use of it, not to mention the development of technology for military purposes.

Technology also encompasses entertainment, and here my father would be most despairing. Our 'smart' televisions allow visual quality to a degree hitherto undreamed of. And we are often advised at the top of our screens about the content of the movies we wish to see: 'self-harm, sex, language, violence, injury detail, drug misuse, threat'. (It is hard to decide whether such 'advice' is offered as a warning to the more sensitive of viewers, or as a recommendation.) My father's reaction to this may be measured by what happened when he took me to see a Western. Westerns in those days had their fair share of shootouts, but movies did not contain as much violence as they do now and violence was far from graphic, most of it being left to the imagination, if the imagination wished to feed upon it, which it usually didn't. The Western finished and it was time for the B movie, which happened to be *Jailhouse Rock.* As soon as Elvis started to contort himself on stage, my father stood up, took my hand and ushered me out of the cinema.

Nowadays, of course, Elvis's sexually orientated contortions would be considered quite conservative, and, in fairness, my father was a victim of his time as each of us is a victim of our own. But at least we can quite accurately gauge how my father would react to 'sex' on the big screen or a screen of any size. He would consider this a species of popular voyeurism and a definite negative. The visualisation of sex in the context of love is one thing, but sex for its own sake is quite another, and I feel certain that my father would want to make the distinction. In the past, sex was left to the imagination, but the effect of making it habitually explicit is to make it a commonplace, and not only a commonplace but an entity in itself unrelated to love or any deep and powerful passion with the exception of lust. 'Lust at first sight' has merged with 'love at first sight', so that separating them has become a herculean feat.

I cannot know whether my father had read Augustine's *Confessions,* but he would have agreed with the advice Augustine gave, as I recall, to a young friend, to the effect that once exposed to the blood lust of the gladiatorial games it is almost certain to become a norm in one's psyche, and once entrenched it is hard if not impossible to free oneself from it. What was true in the fourth century is no less true today, simply because that fickle entity called 'human nature' has not undergone a fundamental change for the better. The more violence is indulged for its own sake, the more acceptable it becomes, and to the most vulnerable, whose number is legion, it becomes a reasonable and relatively easy means of achieving one's goals.

Much the same can be said of the indulgence in sex for its own sake. Sex for its own sake is hardly a new phenomenon, nor would we wish to deny it an important role in the maintenance of good health, but what is relatively new is the way in which the development of technology has made its dissemination so easy and so wide. Sex for its own sake is now taken for granted, such that it has become an essential element in storytelling on the small screen and the big screen and in literature. If your story is short on sex and violence, it is not likely to do very well, and a movie which fails to pay sufficient homage to these two gods is not likely to be a box-office success. The abundant inclusion of these elements is taken very much for granted. We should be wary of taking sex and violence for granted for they are capable of biting the hand that feeds them. Women must not be treated as mere sex objects, yet as these words are written the abuse of women is very much on the increase, as is knife crime in our once relatively peaceful cities, towns and villages.

There are too many cars, too much violence, too much disrespect both for people and for language, and these last two are connected. Mediocrity, which again has inevitably benefitted from the development of technology, rules to a greater extent than ever before. Mediocrity? Well, agreed, excellence has never been and can never be the norm. But mediocrity is capable of masking and supplanting excellence by the sheer weight of numbers, of influence, of sweet persuasion. What is called 'bad language' certainly has a place in our lexis, but if there is little room for anything else we can expect poverty of thought and of feeling. If it is no longer fashionable to speak well, we have lost far more than an alternative lexis. 'Speaking well' becomes downgraded, and what is downgraded tends to be neglected, and what is neglected tends to be forgotten. The richness and variety of language suffers, and with it the expression of thought and feeling.

My father would be appalled by the fact that language has been so cruelly manhandled all in the name of 'coolness', 'fashion' and 'a refusal to be priggish'. It reminds me of the man who complained of his friends who thought him a show-off, 'Whenever I refer to something I've read, or whenever I correct myself or when I'm trying to find a better word, or whenever I give them a good answer to a question, they think I'm showing off. And I dare not refer to the classics!' It seems then that if you wish to keep your friends you'd better do as they do, say as they do and think and feel and as do. This is a prescription that I can, being all too human, well understand, but one that I should do my very best to resist.

It was recently suggested to me that human civilisation is in decline and that it is entering a new Dark Age which will collapse under its own weight. Whether my father would use these words I cannot say, but, after taking a good look around, I think he might well agree with the sentiment. If he dared to quote either from the Bible or from Bunyan's *Pilgrim's Progress*, two books which meant so much to him, I rather think he would be ostracised.

My time is not his time. But there is a kind of continuity of values in the judgements we both make. For what would worry him, worries his son also, which is why I can easily imagine his grave disappointment, which would be piled on top of his grief in having lost his wife, an old lady degraded by dementia, and his awkwardness in speaking to his son, a man 30 years older than he was when he himself ceased to be.

If I speak of a continuity of values, I assume that these values are the importance of liberty of thought and expression, the dignity or indeed sanctity of human life, compassion, the rule of law, an emphasis on tolerance and mutual respect for differences that do not impinge upon the foregoing, understanding and genuine sympathy and a willingness to help or support others in need which may broadly be called 'a sense of humanity'. It is hard to list such values without sounding banal and platitudinous, but there seems little alternative if one wishes to distinguish these 'positive' values from the 'destructive' values that define tyranny, dictatorship, greed, selfishness, genocide and, in a phrase, 'man's inhumanity to man'.

In the continuity of such values lies the importance of literature, in that what worries the writer worries the reader also, or what the reader sees in himself he sees also in the writer. Writers and their readers may therefore shake hands even though centuries separate them. A reader may find a friend in the pages he turns more easily than he would one of flesh and blood in the busy streets he walks abroad. In humbler ways, the letters written between friends or even strangers may also help affirm a concordance of values – perhaps I should say the letters people *used to write*, because, nowadays, laziness, an element on the debit side of human nature, together with the facilitation of the means of communication afforded by the deity of technology, has ensured that letter writing is a lost art (and to think it was once a significant form of literary accomplishment!). No wonder communication between humans has lost most of the depth it once quite often had.

But the fact that we are entitled to speak of a continuity of values at all suggests that we have some grounds for hope that such a continuity will extend into a future which, although perhaps bleak, will not yet be even bleaker. A light that flickers in the corner of a dark room may be better than no light at all.

And as for the development of what we have come to call Artificial Intelligence, he might well wonder what place can be envisaged for human civilisation as distinct from a civilisation of machines. I doubt very much whether he would be loud in singing the praises of human contrivance and technological innovation, since the track record leaves so very much to be regretted. His experience of the technology of war gave him enough to consider. After Hiroshima and Nagasaki, there is much that human beings should ponder and too much that has not yet been pondered. If machines can do all the human can do and do it all infinitely better, we might then see a decline in human ingenuity and the rise of a superior non-human race of beings, though the word 'superior' is not one to be taken lightly, nor is it one that should inspire confidence. There is a certain and terrible irony in any talk of the advancement of human civilisation. Human beings are reliably unreliable, and yet more often than not they can be relied upon to get things wrong. The enthusiasts amongst them repeatedly fail to control the beasts they create, and so Frankenstein's monster roams untamed, while the more credulous amongst them remain blissfully unaware of the danger posed by the next Trojan Horse. Artificial Intelligence is loudly proclaimed by some politicians, who know next to nothing about it, and some experts, who know much less than they profess; both forget that the phenomenon on which they pin such high hopes is very much in its infancy and is in relation to its future development rather akin to a human foetus is to a fully developed adult – the foetus is far less to be feared than the adult which it will become. Politicians see AI as a golden opportunity to boost economic growth through the roof, while its scientific proponents consider it a wonderful and inevitable step towards a utopian age of science. The faith in science is as unfounded as that in 'economic growth', for utopia is far removed from both – as far as human nature itself is removed from perfection. Yet only time and grave error is capable of shaking such a faith, and then, once shaken, it will begin anew in the same or another form. Churchill once remarked that a man will stumble on the truth, get up, shake himself down, and continue on his way. So it is with whole generations.

Would my father, restored to life like Lazarus, agree with all or any of this? I think so. Would his younger self, in the portrait, agree likewise? I cannot say, for there was still much that the younger man was to see and hear, and he would see and hear more than he wanted in the war in which he would be participating.

We can distinguish between a thing in itself and the degree to which that thing exists, and perhaps both the younger and the older man would agree that the distinction makes sense and is well worth making. It is the number of cars, the frequency of bad language, of violence, of disrespect, of aggression, of conflict, of discord, and the breadth and depth of hatred that is of legitimate concern. It is chimerical to hope that these things in themselves should cease to exist, for this must mean that human beings must cease to be what they are, must cease to be human.

Or would they be replaced by machines, and are machines really that dependable? Can anything be done about the *degree* to which these things exist? Does this question make sense? If so, what should be done and is it too late to do it? But are humans themselves to be trusted to do anything about it without falling foul of the very vices which have blackened the history of human life on this planet: bigotry, dictatorship, tyranny – for these are the handmaidens of man's inhumanity to man, the very thing that humans should strive to overcome!

These questions and this whole discussion is riddled with imponderables.

But they are precisely the kind of imponderables that I believe preoccupied my father following his experience of war and up until his own demise. It is this on which my admiration and respect for him is founded, as it would be for anyone who is similarly preoccupied. Imponderables are mired in the doubts and uncertainties to which they give rise.

I say again: imponderables are mired in the doubts and uncertainties to which they give rise. There is no shame attached to doubts and uncertainties of this kind. On the contrary, they are the mark of someone who *lives* as well as breathes, for it seems to me that not all who breathe also live. I refer here to sensitivity and to degrees of sensitivity. It is the kind of bittersweet sensitivity that is discernible in the interview with Pablo Casals, in his reply to the question, 'At 95 years of age, do you still have hopes and dreams?' His answer is not a simple yes or no. Instead, he refers to the beauty of symmetry and form of plants and flowers. We must draw uncertain conclusions from this reply, but the most compelling of these conclusions is that here speaks a man of exceptional sensitivity, the kind of sensitivity that compels a man to ask imponderable questions about the human condition and how it might be improved. Imponderable questions will necessarily have inconclusive answers. Simply, there are some questions which have no answers. And here we are bound to ask whether such questions are really questions at all, or something else merely masquerading as questions because they are incapable of taking any other form short of an inarticulate sound or a guttural groan resembling that of pain. The sensitivity to frame such questions and the courage to suffer uncertainty inspires our sympathy and perhaps also a sense of fraternity – a confirmation of a continuity of values, for a rejection of things as they are is really a recommendation that they should change and be replaced by precisely those values whose continuity we wish to assert. The very existence of people like Casals and Mother Teresa is an exemplar of such a continuity, like stars from a distant galaxy, which we have no hope of ever reaching, in our own dark and foreboding skies.

It may be true, as I have suggested, to say that what worried my father worries me also. But this fails to take into account the *degree* to which we both worry, a degree which is affected by the *level of expectation.* This litany, as I have called it, of complaints and objections directed at so-called 'human nature' as it relates to the 'human condition' is either exacerbated or mollified by what can reasonably be expected concerning change and improvement in that nature. Here, I believe, is where my father and I must differ, and the difference between us is founded on his first-hand experience of war as distinct from the second-hand and third-hand accounts I have been given. When, in passing the portrait, I say 'But it isn't Dunkirk, dad!' to express the fact that my worries about something or other are nothing in comparison, I really have little or no idea what I am saying, little or no idea of how true this statement is.

My father's first-hand experience of the horror of war may well have been expected to lower his expectations of what can be asked of the human nature that was fundamentally its cause. True, the forces of good overcame the forces of evil, if we may be allowed an optimistic oversimplification. But the price paid for this was astronomical in terms of human life and suffering. Victory was at least bittersweet and the end of conflict was short-lived. While people danced in Trafalgar Square, unthinkable destruction in Hiroshima and Nagasaki, followed by the war in Korea, still loomed, to say nothing of the Cold War which presented fearful prospects if the temperature rose, and conflict in Palestine lay ahead – never a moment in which one could seriously say that war on this planet was at an end. Other inhumanities emanating from the partition of Germany and the insufferably poor conditions in which survivors of Berlin and many other cities ravaged by disease and crime found themselves added to the grief of unfixable personal loss and deprivation.

One reason why the elderly find it hard to survive retirement is that they switch on their televisions for some form of entertainment only to find violence, crime and aggression, not simply in movies but on the news channels, not just in fiction but in reality – a constant stream of bloodletting and a cascade of inhumanities. Better to buy a puppy and go for endless walks in the park than to depend on the credit side of human nature to ease the boredom of a life without work.

But suffice to say that my expectations concerning the credit side of human nature, though indeed bereft of a sufficiency of hope, are nevertheless markedly less despairing than my father's could reasonably be expected to be after his own experience of war and in view of events and conditions either consequent upon it or almost immediately following it. It is one thing to sit comfortably by the fireside listening to the accounts given by Old Jack of war in the trenches and quite another to actually experience them, one thing to see a corpse in a movie and quite another to see those of your comrades in a state of putrefaction in No Man's Land.

If we speak of expectations, it is a question of what one believes can and what one believes cannot be reasonably expected from human beings. This is important, because the wrong level of expectations can play havoc with those sensitive souls who dare to think deeply about the 'human condition' or, more precisely, feel totally and morally constrained to think about it, whether they will or not.

We may consider the views of the Cambridge philosopher Bertrand Russell as a case in point. Here was a man who had thought deeply about the human condition, but his contemplation took place in circumstances that were markedly more comfortable than either the trenches of the first world war or the rubble of the cities of the second, as I am sure he would agree. In one of his interviews he was asked what advice he would give to future generations. He had two pieces of advice, one which he called 'intellectual' and the other he called 'moral'. We might do well to consider them.

18

BERTRAND RUSSELL AND OLD JACK

Although the interview in question took place in the comfortable surroundings of his study, it should be remembered that Russell was no armchair moralist or social commentator. He attended marches and sit-down demonstrations in protest against multilateral nuclear disarmament, and he was even prepared to be imprisoned for his belief, which in fact happened for a short period in his 90s. Having given him due credit for his willingness to practice what he preached, there is nevertheless something too comfortably academic or hypothetical, not to say fanciful, about the advice, both intellectual and moral, that he wishes to give to future generations.

The intellectual advice he gives is really a plea for objectivity when considering any issue. He tells us to consider the facts, not what we would like them to be but what they really are. The word 'fact' has a wide currency and seems simple enough, but a philosophical analysis of the concept 'fact' might leave you with the impression that it is anything but simple. Leaving such analyses aside, we may at least say that there is, in everyday life, very often a disagreement about what the facts are in any given situation. Moreover, the facts are coloured by our interpretations, prejudices, beliefs, convictions, dogmas, preferences and experiences, so that we are predisposed to consider a fact someone else might consider unproven, disputable or even plainly untrue. Did A kill B? But did he murder him? Or assassinate him? Or allow him to die? If he allowed him to die, is it right to say that he killed him? If he assassinated him, is it right to say that he murdered him? And if A ran over B in his car, are any of these questions appropriate? The essential and perhaps indisputable fact, you might say, is that A killed B. Even so, our understanding of this fact is coloured by the circumstances in which it is, as it were, embedded, which is why the law is bound to take these circumstances into account.

Russell was, of course, well aware of all this. Nevertheless, his plea for objectivity asks a very great deal. It is the kind of objectivity that one academic has the right to expect of another in academia. Even then, perfect objectivity might be chimerical, something to be aimed at, certainly, but only ever imperfectly achieved. But the *striving* for it is important. It supposes a willingness to put yourself outside your own convictions, beliefs, and, perhaps, culture, the platitudes of your own upbringing, and, well, *outside yourself*! And one of the greatest obstacles to this is emotion. Your emotional involvement in a situation may be so deep as to preclude the kind of detachment that Russell's prescription requires. In situations which involve immediate personal loss, for example, and consequent and lasting grief, a Buddhistic degree of detachment can't reasonably be expected. Even when emotions are as cold as ice, it is hard, and for most people quite impossible, to suspend, let alone question, the beliefs with which they have been brought up and often brainwashed. Bedrock beliefs and prejudices are hard to remove without an intellectual surgery so radical as to threaten the patient's very survival.

The kind of detachment and objectivity that Russell so commendably prescribes is just unrealistic over a wide area of fundamental issues, and therefore people will continue to misconstrue the facts, invent facts where they have no independent existence, or colour them from the paint box they were given as children, or simply disregard them altogether. Indeed, facts may be disregarded altogether, or coloured in such a way that their outlines are blurred and hardly discernible, even when the historical evidence for the conventional description of them is so overwhelming and so indisputable that to either deny or alter them may be considered starkly insane. (There are 'historians' who deny that the Holocaust ever took place, and 'eccentrics' who believe that the Earth is flat!)

Commendable though it is, and despite the fact that there are of course many occasions when we should all try to do better to question and at least temporarily suspend our deepest prejudices, Russell's prescription for objectivity smacks of wishful thinking. But that we should *try* to do better, is perhaps all that Russell means, and most rational and basically decent people would probably agree with him when it is put to them, provided their emotions are sufficiently cooled, and preferably when they believe that God's in his Heaven and all's right with the world.

The *desire* to be objective, the wish to subject one's own feelings to scrutiny, to see things more clearly or to submit one's worldview to criticism, is like *wanting* to see things from another's point of view. But it takes a very good and very rare person to feel as strongly as this. It is almost a religious or spiritual conviction. For most people who find themselves in the most trying of circumstances, it is a feeling that can only be aspired to, never attained.

Russell calls this piece of advice 'intellectual'. Rightly, because it belongs to those who attach value to the intellect and to an intellectual understanding of the world, a perception of the world that endeavours to put emotions to one side in favour of reason – the old dichotomy raises its head yet again. The world is not overpopulated with intellectuals, most people being moved much of the time by their emotions and half-baked ideas and too many people exclusively so when it comes to profound global issues and perceived human rights and perceived injustices. Russell's perception that gives reason primacy over feeling accords perfectly with Russell as the author of *Principia Mathematica*, for there is no room for the emotions in mathematical reasoning. Russell might give us the impression that he tends to see factual statements as though they were the propositions of mathematics. Russell would not of course make such a ridiculous equation. But we may perhaps be forgiven for thinking his view of objectivity as unrealistically cold, mechanical and impersonal – a 'mathematical' objectivity, one that is far too 'objective' in the world of political, moral and personal facts!

Much more might be said on this matter, but we must forbear and turn next to Russell's 'moral' prescription, which is summed up by saying 'Love is wise, hatred is foolish'. His point is that in the world of today, much smaller than that of the past and burdened with nuclear weapons, we should endeavour to tolerate one another. There are many things others might say that we find offensive, but, he says, if we wish to live together and not die together, we must learn a kind of tolerance. Such advice, if said quickly enough, might pass muster if the issues which divide the world and its peoples were not so acute, not so deep, not so persistent. Even if we were to allow what people say, we cannot always allow what they do. There must be limits to what people are allowed to do, and often what they do can be expected to follow from what they say, and what they do if frequently of a kind that can hardly be expected to be forgiven. Granted that there must be limits to what can be tolerated, but within those limits, there is still much that we can do, or try to do, to tolerate far more than we do. But that being said, if Russell were alive today, he may well say that many societies have become almost neurotically obsessed with saying the right thing, and not saying the wrong thing, even to the extent that 'free speech' can never be granted or tolerated without inverted commas, for free speech must now pass the litmus test of political correctness. Sensitivity and 'making allowances for present company' is hardly a new or unacceptable prescription, but human beings can rarely be trusted to act in moderation, and things might easily reach a point at which even cautiously-minded people are afraid to make valid contributions to discussions of weighty matters. The result is the demise of free speech, except perhaps in name, while freedom of thought continues to exist only until, if the day ever comes, our thoughts are made readable by others! Sensitivity is commendable and indispensable in a morally civilised world, but it is indeed possible to have too much of a good thing. In other words, human beings are very apt to make a complete hash of the very best of things.

Toleration of what others say and do is not at all easy, and sometimes it is not at all possible. The irony here is that Russell is prescribing toleration in circumstances that are most grave, the kind of circumstances that he himself could never tolerate. He was opposed to the first world war, believing that the responsibility for the conflagration lay at Britain's door as much as it did at Germany's. But he could never have been a conscientious objector in Hitler's war. He thoroughly supported the fight against Nazism, presumably because he thought, rightly or wrongly, that the issues involved were far graver than those involved in the Kaiser's war. Whether they were graver or not, they were certainly very grave, and he was most assuredly in the right to refuse to tolerate them. But did he think it conceivable before the beginning of either conflict that the different parties involved could really have talked things out, allowed each other's standpoint, reached a compromise and resolved the issues peaceably? This is very much to be doubted concerning the Kaiser, and quite out of the question for the Führer.

No doubt two neighbours quarrelling over whether the garden fence should be higher or lower would benefit for taking tea together and trying their best to reach a sensible compromise. In fact, the recourse to tea and a friendly chat would I think be extremely rare, if not quite saintly. But if one of them were to burn down the fence, it is not at all likely that his viewpoint would earn greater respect than it did before.

Moreover, quarrels between otherwise or erstwhile neighbours are not the kind of conflicts in which Russell is interested. In the context of his advice to future generations, he is of course primarily, if not solely, interested in conflicts and disputes between whole nations, the so-called 'super powers', and those countries which are, almost inevitably, led by tyrants and insane despots with imperialist motivations destined to enhance their power, prestige and untouchability.

Russell's prescriptions, though delightfully pious, well-intended and well-worth giving, bristle with difficulties when it comes to their probable or even possible realisation in the crazy world in which we all live. I say well-worth giving, because they give thinking people great pause for thought about the world in which they live. But if they were to be given to unthinking people, they would sound pretty vacuous and have little or no effect whatsoever.

But what effect might they have on people like my father or Old Jack? Here once again I must guess. I believe they would nod sagely on hearing Russell's prescriptions and agree with him entirely. But for them such prescriptions would be bittersweet, not because such advice fails to stand up to some kind of philosophical analysis or scrutiny, but because they have seen some of the worst behaviour that humans are capable of inflicting upon one another, summed up in the phrase 'the insanity of war'. They would, I believe, regard war as a species of madness, and for this reason Russell's words would sound hollow, for madmen cannot be reasoned with and therefore are not open to the rational possibility of compromise. Moreover, there is no such thing as a moral appeal to the sanctity of human life and the inhumanity of all war, for in madness there is no appeal that can make a difference. Perhaps the only appeal that can ever be successfully made to those who are insane and obnoxious is an appeal that is equally insane or obnoxious. What can I say to someone, believing himself Napoleon, wielding a sword and waiting for the next man to enter the room, convinced that that next man will be Wellington and determined to kill him? I can perhaps convince him that Wellington has already left and is on a train to King's Cross. Then, as Napoleon makes his way to the station to catch the next train to London, I can phone the police and have him apprehended and safely incarcerated. Only an absurd proposition can be made to the insane with any chance of success.

The realisation of Russell's prescriptions are not likely to be considered very likely by my father or Old Jack or indeed by anyone with sufficient experience of war or indeed of life. Had Russell spoken to Plato about war, the latter might well have said that only the dead have seen the end of it. The unlikelihood of a *universal* and totally *inclusive* adoption of Russell's prescriptions should not of course prevent us from arguing the case for it. Something is better than nothing. Indeed, these prescriptions must already be followed to some significant extent, otherwise human life would be far worse than it is or even by now non-existent. Universality and inclusivity would in any case require humans to cease to be what they are, namely *human*. And that requirement deserves a great deal of circumspection.

If the appeal for universality and inclusivity must fall on deaf ears, it is natural that sensitive souls should look elsewhere for succour, consolation and comfort and at least a modicum of hope. My father was brought up to respect his Christian heritage, his own father being a 'fire and brimstone' lay preacher, and his experience of war was no doubt made more bearable by his belief in a Creator who left the world to Satan and promised eternal life to those who followed the teachings given by his Son in the Sermon on the Mount. My father's quiet, gentle demeanour suggests that he was not of the 'fire and brimstone' kind – at least, I prefer to doubt that he was. But he attended a Baptist chapel on Sundays whenever circumstances allowed and sometimes took me with him.

Old Jack attended a Roman Catholic church every Sunday for as long as he was physically able, dressing up for the occasion. Failing to find sufficient grounds for hope amongst humans here on Earth, he perhaps looked to Heaven and the promise of a Day of Reckoning when all tears would be washed away and all those who caused them would be reckoned with. He entertained, as most believers do, a vague notion of justice, of goodness and an eventual paradise on Earth. Such ideas, though necessarily unclear, are nevertheless sufficient to enable those to go on when they say that they can't go on, to continue their struggle when the struggle is over, to fight for causes that seem lost to them, to speak the words of hope when such words have repeatedly proved hollow. Those who speak of God as 'Father' seldom ask themselves what this word is supposed to mean or what such a father might look like. Nor should they. Vagueness is required, for the sentiment is all. The sentiment would not be what it is, would not have the power it has, were the word or words used to describe it capable of specificity. On one very memorable occasion, as Old Jack and I were sitting by the fireside on a bitterly cold and snowy day, I happened to mention that one of the philosophers I had been reading questioned the idea of God as a kind of physical entity and argued that the word 'God' was only the name of an idea. I must have given a very clear explanation of this philosopher's position – far too clear, for the expression on Old Jack's face turned from one of interest to one of dismay. I felt so guilty for upsetting him. I was anxious to change the subject rapidly and did so by dismissing it with 'Well, anyway, it's just an opinion, because nobody knows anything!' Thankfully it did the trick, because Old Jack seemed to brighten up a bit and started to tell me a tale from the trenches which was as far removed from philosophical debate as it is possible to be. I promised myself never to talk about God again, a promise I solemnly kept. Old Jack worshipped a conception of God that was necessarily, inevitably and very delightfully vague. And that's exactly how it should have been. Anything else would have been gratuitously cruel, callous, cynical, unfeeling and unwise.

Because they could hardly put their hopes for the future of humanity into the hands of earthly guardians, they appealed to their God, a loving, caring God, one that was a God of love through and through. But vaguely intermixed with this was also a God that would punish the unjust and bring tyrants and cruel despots to account, indeed all those who were hard-hearted and impervious to the warmth of love – all this on a Day of Judgement.

Did they believe in a Day of Judgement? I am quite unable to say with absolute conviction what either of them did or did not believe. For what men believe or do not believe is hardly ever clear to them either. Suffice to say that they were both good men, which means that neither of them felt at ease in a world that is so full of hatred and its ugly offspring.

I feel pity for men like my father and Old Jack for experiencing first-hand what I have never experienced and certainly hope never to experience in the few years that might lie ahead. For all such men have seen the worst that humans can do, not forgetting that the worst is not confined to the battlefield, not forgetting either that the worst is not limited to the dealings between men but includes also the unspeakable cruelty meted out by parents to their own children, and the innumerable inhumanities that take place on the 'civilised' streets of our 'civilised' cities, and the subtle cruelties in marriages between those who have no liking for each other but only a dislike that love, if it exists at all, is unable to temper let alone overcome, for disliking someone you love is a very common phenomenon.

I say I feel pity for those who have first-hand experience of war. It is not difficult to feel deeply about the whole of mankind, and the feeling helps to temper what would otherwise be an unqualified condemnation of all who walk on two legs. To live is not easy. We cannot live without others, some of whom will define our own existence, give us our identity. But neither is it easy to live with others, with people who have their own ideas, their own perception of their wants and needs, their rights and obligations, many of which will conflict with our own, or what we perceive our own to be, for we all make mistakes, some of which are very costly and painful. And then there is personal loss and the grief entailed. Pity for those who have first-hand experience of war must also extend to those who have experience of poverty, hunger and disease, of great loss, of disillusionment and of bitter disappointment. Whatever else it may be, life is painful – a fact which must surely give us pause before we bring children into such a world, and a fact which causes us no little discomfort when we think of the children we leave behind when our own lives draw to a close.

The pity uppermost in mind here, however, is that for my father and Old Jack, burdened as they must have been with memories they would not have wished for, ones they could never relinquish. Who could seriously reproach them for smoking their cigarettes and pipes? The balm against the miseries within must have been in very short supply. Not even those who loved them most could offer much in the way of forgetfulness and the resurrection of hope.

19

IN PRAISE OF DREAMFUL SLEEP

Sleep did not come easy to my father in his latter years, when his hair was receding, his complexion was grey and his frowns deeper. I painfully recall his moans and groans of discomfort as I, perhaps still afraid of the dark, lay awake in the adjacent room, wondering when and how it was all going to end. I had little conception of death, but I remember being lulled to sleep with a sense of impending loss. Life without my father was inconceivable, but, young as I was, I knew things couldn't go on like that forever.

I cannot say what dreams my father had or whether he dreamed at all when eventually he fell asleep. The nature of dreams was one of the many subjects that we would never be able to discuss around the breakfast table. Being an experienced dreamer myself, I hate to think what unpleasant nights my father might have had, wanting sleep to come but afraid of what dark and frightful images it might conjure up when it did.

Socrates, in Plato's *Apology*, philosophises about death. He says that if death is total unconsciousness, like a dreamless sleep, it would be a great boon, 'For if a man had to choose that night in which he slept so soundly as not even to dream, and, after comparing it with all the other nights and days of his life, had, after due deliberation, to say how many days and nights in his life he had spent more pleasantly and happily than this, I think that not only a private person, but even the Great King* himself would find such nights easy to count in comparison with the other nights and days. If then death is like this, I count it a gain: for thus reckoned, all eternity seems no longer than a single night.' (* i.e. the King of Persia.)

Those that wear the crown must bear its weight, and so we may presume that those in high places would prefer a dreamless sleep to a sleep full of frightful dreams, a sleep full of nightmares, of worrisome shapes and grotesquely unfamiliar places, of threats and horror-filled challenges, for sufficient unto the daylight are the evils thereof.

But suppose, instead, that as distinct from life lived during the anxiety-ridden hours of daylight involving feelings of *real* grief from *real* loss, dreams offered an alternative life, an additional life, a parallel universe of consciousness, one of sweetness offering an opportunity to meet again those who have gone before, those one has admired and loved. Such a life would be a paradise to be welcomed without reservation, in comparison to which one's waking hours would seem dull and painful. With the Bard we might then say with unparalleled passion, 'Sleep, sleep, perchance to dream!'

Socrates says that death might be like this, in that it allows us to meet again those we have loved and lost.

But if sweet dreams could give us an additional consciousness, we could have two lives, one in the daylight hours and one in the hours of darkness in the world of dreams, the latter even making the former more pleasant than otherwise, for during the daylight hours we could know that we shall soon meet our loved ones again during the hours of sweetening sleep.

Nonsense? Yes, if swallowed whole. But, like the Curate's Egg, it is wholesome in part. If you dream of a lost loved one and the dream is sweet, is that a bad or a pleasant experience? The latter, I should think. You might then tell yourself that they are still with you, that they have not entirely ceased to exist, that they are there somewhere in the ether, or at least in the ether of dreams. And you would be right. If they talk to you in your dreams, you may still hold a conversation with them, be guided by them, be comforted by them.

I say this because I have never, not even once in all these years, dreamed about my father, never seen him in my sleep let alone held a conversation with him or been guided by him or been comforted by him. Dreams I have certainly had, especially in more recent years, but they have been mostly unwelcome, involving the unpleasant and the unfamiliar, leaving me, when awake, feeling distraught and vaguely anxious. Among the few pleasant dreams I've had, my father takes no part in them, he plays not even so much as a cameo role. People ask what dreams tell us and that to ignore a dream is like refusing to read a letter sent through the mists of sleep and addressed to you alone – unwise, they say, for such dispatches, like photographs, can never lie. Perhaps there are ways in which dreams, like photographs, can indeed lie. My maternal grandmother used to say that the truth is always opposite to what a bad dream depicts – but no doubt she said this to put my mind at rest after my nightmares. Nevertheless, perhaps dream letters do have a lot to tell us if only we knew how to read them, and so it may be unwise to pay them no heed.

But if we should ask what dreams have to tell us, should we not also ask what *not* having dreams tells us? In particular, what does not having dreams about someone so deeply loved and so deeply missed tell us? Why have I never dreamed about my own father, or never dreamed a dream in which he somehow features? Does it say something about me, or him? Perhaps it says nothing at all. Are we intellectually prepared for such blind-alley answers?

Imponderables apart, I can at least say that whatever power or influence my father has had in recent years does not come overtly from my dreams or enter into them in any recognisable shape or form.

It comes from the portrait that hangs on the wall on the landing. The portrait that speaks and listens and puts words into my head does everything that a dream could do; only better, because dreams carry with them ambiguities and obscurities that are open doors to all kinds of interpretations or no interpretation at all. The words that it puts into my head I have already put into its mouth, and the fact that it listens and that it speaks is by my leave. I have given it the life that seems separate from my own. Yet it does have an identity separate from my own, because the life that I have given it derives from what I remember about the man the portrait depicts, things said and done by the man himself, fragments that belong to a formal biography but are also far removed from one. My father has the dignity and the status that I give him because he had thoroughly earned it. It was not a fabrication pasted on by an overactive and wishful-thinking imagination. In the portrait he was less than half the age he was when he died, but the portrait contains the seeds of the man he was to become, shaped by war, shaped by the trammels of life and his inevitable and, I should say, inconclusive reflections on the human condition.

The so-called power of the portrait is the sense of presence it invokes. Yet that presence is not confined to its location on the wall on the landing. It is a presence that is felt anywhere and everywhere when all is silent, when the air is undefiled by the soundwaves of television and radio and smartphones and laptop computers. When all is quiet, so quiet that the sound of silence seems threatening and alarming. Perhaps the silence is broken by a bird song or a dry leaf that falls from a tree tinkling down through the hedge below, events that only accentuate the silence that reigns before and after. In the silence of cold and unfamiliar places the presence of the face in the portrait is most felt, because then it is most needed. The face in the portrait cannot speak until I will it to do so, and it is in silences that seem hostile that I seek its voice most. The portrait now gives voice to the words I hear at such times, yet that voice predates the portrait and was heard long before the photograph was enlarged and framed and installed on the landing where I now live. And that voice which predates the portrait belonged to the man whose decline and demise I remember so vividly.

It was the voice I heard one unforgettable day two or three years after my father's passing. Like many teenagers I craved a gun to carry on a shoulder strap as I walked the hills, perhaps pretending to be some explorer in forests bristling with danger. The hills were, and I have no doubt still are, lonely, silent places. A gentle wind would occasionally bend the grass, and the occasional skylark might rise, flutter and escape the sound of human tread, a sheep in a distant place might bleat, but for the most part everywhere was silent, a silence that might inspire either poetry or flight. In me it inspired reflection, reflection on my father's demise, on my mother's inconsolable grief and on my own. The future seemed far away and no better than the present and the promise that time would heal the wounds of loss seemed hollow. The thought occurred to me that I might turn the gun on myself and, in an instant, end it all. I say, the thought occurred to me – a mere thought, not at all a serious intention, but it seemed to me so easy and so permanent a solution. I had recently heard of a local boy who died accidentally after a gun was pointed at him and the trigger was pulled in jest and in the certain belief that the gun was not loaded. The gun had been a birthday present which the boy had proudly shown to his friend – the friend who pointed it at him and pulled the trigger. I thought of this and of how easy it would be to annihilate one's consciousness and be free of pain. It should have occurred to me that in death one is free of everything, pleasure as well as pain, and that the idea that death is simply an eternal sleep plays the devil with us all. If death is simply anything, it is simply nothing at all. But it is hard to conceive of one's own non-existence, and Montaigne's prescription to think of the time before one's birth does not really cut it.

But I do remember thinking the obvious, namely that the gun that had killed that boy was the same kind of gun that I now held in my hands to do my bidding, namely a 0.410 calibre shotgun, which happened to be loaded with a magnum cartridge. (It was the same gun with which I had managed to bring down a bird in flight. It had been a long shot and I remember feeling proud that I had managed to do it in one. My pride was short-lived as I approached the bird, which had fallen some distance into the long grass. It was not yet dead, and it looked at me pleadingly as if to say, 'But why?' In all these years I have never managed to forget that poor bird, and I still charge myself with murder to this day. The image of that bird haunts me even now, a fact which no doubt many would consider ample proof of my lack of manliness and adult moral backbone.)

While I contemplated with what ease I might rid myself of the world or rid the world of me, the voice that belonged to my deceased father forced entry into my head like an invigorated Counsel for the Prosecution, accusing me of forgetting that the effect of ceasing to exist would be far too much for my poor mother to bear, that I had a responsibility towards her, and that the future might not yet be as bleak for either of us as I now imagined it to be. I suppose I faintly nodded in acquiescence as the gentle breeze still caused the grass to bend and some distant sheep bleated in agreement. In any case, I ejected the magnum cartridge, returned it to my pocket unfired, shouldered the gun and walked the long walk home to my mother and less-hostile surroundings. I do not say that my father's case for the Prosecution saved me from a premature ending, for I do not think that I had seriously contemplated putting the idea of self-extinction into effect. But his words had succeeded in turning my thoughts away from myself and reminding me of my responsibility towards another, a responsibility that was born of love as distinct from a cold sense of duty. Naturally, it may be said that I would have lacked the courage to pull the trigger on myself anyway even if I had really intended to do so – well, that is a point I would not entirely discount, but what 'courage' is supposed to mean in such a case is not immediately clear. Perhaps what I would have lacked, instead, is the requisite foolishness to do the deed, for the word 'courage' is one that I would rather reserve for a far nobler sacrifice. No, the point of recalling this whole episode is to emphasise that the voice I heard in my head removed a selfish preoccupation with myself and replaced it with a reminder of my mother's sufferings and, perhaps, of her hopes for a brighter future, out there, somehow and somewhere on an admittedly vague horizon. A spark is not yet a flame, and a flame is not yet a fire, but a fire may begin with a spark, and I suppose I saw it as my responsibility to give every chance to that spark to light the tinder. My own extinction would have removed the tinder and therefore every possibility of even a hope-on-crutches.

What does this intervention of the voice say that has not already been said but said poorly? Is it not the voice of a role model that is deeply loved and justly revered?

If all that I am trying to say were to take the form of a sculpture, embarrassingly crude and a whole galaxy removed from a Michael Angelo, it might be said to be 'A Study in Grief', an instance of the species of grief that is the inevitable price of love – the kind of grief that must be distinguished from a prolonged indulgence in painful reflection solely for the sake of attention-seeking morbidity.

The night my father died, my mother and I swore that we would stick together forever, which, of course, is a promise that cannot possibly be kept. But the promise meant that together we could at least continue to live somehow. And we did continue to live, giving each other mutual support and held fast and permanently together by the shared memories of the man who had been husband and father. When my mother died, my wife and children were my chief supports, without whom her passing would have been emotionally crippling and pushed me into a state of permanent resentment for a second loss so great. The need for the support of others is universal and fundamental, and much, I am tempted to say gratuitous, difficulty comes from a deficiency of it and, too often, from its total absence. It is, I hope, quite needless to say that when my mother eventually died, she was the last link in a chain of memories of my father. Her death was a reminder that some promises that cannot be kept are nevertheless worth making. But her demise made me half again of what I was before. The half that remained was and is supported by my wife and children, and by a conviction that even those who live 'fractionally' may yet have something worthwhile to do and to say precisely because they live with a persistent sense of loss.

It is impossible to write about my father and his impact upon me without also thinking of my mother when we lived together after his demise. On warm summer days I think of the cheap, simple dresses and skirts she wore, and on winter days I think of how cold that ground-floor council flat was, with a central heating system that didn't work and an oil stove that had to be lit every morning with shaking hands attached to a shivering body – getting dressed for school was a living nightmare. 'Dress quickly and you'll be alright,' she would say, and I did my best to follow her advice to the extent that the process came to resemble an

Olympic event. 'Switch off that light if you don't need it,' she'd say, and this has given me a keen sense of needless usage that has lasted the rest of my life, and possibly beyond. I have already mentioned Christmas, which every year was a bittersweet prospect, and a flat which couldn't be heated properly or for long enough made matters worse. No serious attempt was made by the council authorities to fix the heating problem, and it ceased to be an issue only when we moved elsewhere. It feels as though things have turned full circle. At the time of writing, the present and misnamed Labour government has axed the already inadequate Winter Fuel Allowance for the elderly, many of whom huddle over candles with their hands in mittens.

These snippets of life with my mother are important for what they omit. Perhaps I have already said enough, but it is worth repeating that she was obliged to become a fighter, that she at all times took care of her clothes and appearance, and that she was a straight talker, not as sharp and expressive as Betsey Trotwood, David Copperfield's famous aunt, but nevertheless someone who loved the company of others provided it was always on her own terms. It was very easy to outstay your welcome with my mother. But she was as sensitive and kindhearted as she was straight, and she bore her troubles bravely and kept up appearances right to the end. Her lack of higher education saved her from the more common forms of pretension it usually engenders. It gave her an earthy wisdom and helped keep her sincere and down to earth, virtues which I have respected even more since her passing. She retained, or developed, an attractive sense of humour despite, or because of, her persistent grief and sense of insecurity. All in all, and when she was in her prime and at her best, she was someone to admire and respect. In the last decade of her life her mental decline weakened her and many of her virtues were smothered in a heavy cloak of deterioration and were consequently hidden from view. With people like Socrates, Casals and my father she stands as a worthy role model and the very small world she inhabited is infinitely poorer for her loss.

I pity all those who have no good men or women to respect and admire and count myself fortunate to have known a few souls that I can at least aspire to follow. I also count myself fortunate that I somehow have the ability to recognise those things that are worthy of praise and that I have the desire, though not perhaps the capacity, to emulate the qualities that I so heartily commend. The ability to recognise commendable qualities must be supposed to come from the examples set by others, just as blindness to what is commendable must come from the profusion of bad examples and from the fact that bad examples are in the habit of becoming acceptable, or at least too easily expected, norms of behaviour. When what, I believe, G.K. Chesterton called a feeling of 'virgin astonishment' towards evil waxes and wanes, bad examples become all too common instances of things that are viewed with an unfortunate degree of acceptance. (At this point I feel that philosophising is in danger of impinging upon common sense and shall therefore refrain from further comment.)

Suffice to say, I have been fortunate to have known, or to have known of, some good people in a bad world. I can only hope for the same for my children who must continue after me in a world that becomes more difficult by the day. Hopefully they will find role models worthy of emulation, some guiding lights, some outstretched hand, a moral compass that can be trusted to point north in all circumstances. It is important to remember the obvious, that role models are human beings. Hope must lie with humans, not with machines. Only humans can feel hope and express hope, and only humans can lose it. I suppose that is what I see in the portrait of my more youthful father, the fresh, smiling face of a young man who was soon to see just how bad the world can be, just how cruel people can be to each other. Perhaps that is why I salute it every time I pass it, and speak to it and for it, in the hope that for all he came to experience, that hope was, though battered and torn, never entirely lost. His smile is greeted by my own, I smile to his smile, I recognise the hope expressed there. I prefer to believe that, despite everything, that smile was never lost. Ah, yes, it is also a *knowing* smile, a *sober* smile, but a smile nonetheless. It belongs to a man who started up in the stars, was taken down to the very depths, and then rose up again. It is the very embodiment of Bunyan's sentiment which, for the very last time, I shall repeat, 'Be ye watchful, and cast away fear; be sober, and hope to the end.'

Yes, but then…

20

THERE IS HOPE, AND THERE IS HOPE

Since we have blithely quoted Bunyan several times, the key word 'hope' is well worth an investigation. For not all hope is on the same level. Hope is a house of many mansions, which means that it is of many kinds. Bunyan deserves our attention lest we fall prey to treating his prescription as no more than a comforting mantra without understanding what it is that consoles or comforts us. And here we should remember that a little realism and a little intellectual honesty may be painful. But despite many things I see and hear around me, I still believe that the pursuit of truth is a noble enterprise. Besides, the portrait nods assent.

Bunyan is not talking about what we may term 'solely personal, or material or circumstantial hope'. You may hope for a better job, for a raise, for a better car, and the young may hope to get married and start a family, and others may hope that their children get a better start in life, or you may hope for a change in the weather so that you can enjoy your weekend break, while others may hope that the operation is successful and that they'll be free of pain at last. This is already a mixed bag, but all such hopes are of course perfectly valid.

But although all hope presupposes uncertainty concerning outcomes, the hope that Bunyan is interested in is impersonal and distinctly moral and has more to do with the establishment of Heaven on Earth, and such a hope encompasses the hope that there might one day be an end to all war, all aggressive and cruel divisions, all moral injustices. And hope of this kind and of this generality or universality opens the door to faith, with or without a capital 'F', and here we have further division.

People of Faith, though they differ on points of doctrine, may agree that their God has a plan. They may believe in a Day of Judgement when the wicked shall be punished and the earth will be cleansed thereby and Jerusalem finally established. In the meantime, the good can aspire to Heaven and the bad can expect eternal damnation, for there is always an Afterlife as a kind of intermediate form of consolation. The belief might be that a loving God made humans in his image but that they transmuted after Adam and Eve's transgression and that God left them to it, giving Satan hegemony over mankind. Man is therefore faced with a battle against Dark Forces, with a war which is unwinnable unless through complete submission to the Divine Will or through God's grace.

Ask people of Faith to explain the tenets of their belief and you will find as many answers as there are questions. For in such matters as this, they are forever attempting to hit a moving target, and there is no way of knowing whether the mark has been hit. I leave you to draw your own conclusions from this.

It seems, however, that such people of Faith are not placing their hopes on mankind, or on mankind alone to ensure that 'Thy will be done on Earth as it is in Heaven'.

The humanists might say that people of Faith are conjuring up an elaborate mythology at the expense of human capabilities. They might say that a morally superior world can be created by man alone and that people of Faith are underestimating man's moral capacity to generate such a world unaided by fairy stories. People of Faith, they might say, create a gratuitous God at man's expense.

Humanists may also be prone to scientism, which the Oxford dictionary defines as 'an excessive belief in or application of scientific method'. Humanistic mindsets may also be scientistic, and these in turn encompass an exaggerated faith in the 'power of technology'. Humanism, scientism and, let us coin the word, technologism, may therefore be compounded together as a united front against the elevation of a mythical God above human achievement.

It might be wondered what such a Compound has to do with a *morally* superior universe or with the creation of a morally superior world. My own response to this question is that no rational or logical connexion exists whatsoever. And yet, I might be in the minority. Highly intelligent people believe not only that there is a connexion but that the connexion can be taken very much for granted. Patrick Moore, the eminent – and largely self-taught – astrophysicist, believed that were aliens intelligent enough to arrive here on Earth their technological superiority to humans would necessarily be matched by a moral superiority, and the whole idea of war would have been left very far behind them! This view was flatly rejected by Stephen Hawking, who believed that we should give a very wide berth to aliens seeking contact since, he said, their motives would be far from honourable but, on the contrary, exploitative.

If I am right, the truth is that no conclusions whatsoever can be drawn about the moral status of alien life, favourable or otherwise, simply from their technological or scientific capabilities. From the fact that they are scientifically and technologically superior beings, it does not follow that they are either morally better or worse than their human counterparts.

(This kind of discussion is riddled with stark, but perhaps forgivable, simplicities. We talk of 'alien life' as though it were a form of life more or less recognisable as human. The truth is, the phrase 'alien life' in this particular context is quite meaningless.)

People of Faith are thought by their retractors to place too little faith in man, while those who adhere to elements of what we have called the Compound are considered by people of Faith to have raised him too high. And, as I have said, those whose faith lies in the Compound leave out perhaps the most important element of all – a *moral* component.

And yet, it is precisely this moral component that is bound up with Bunyan's use of the word 'hope'.

Moral improvement in human life can accompany any other kinds of improvement, those that are possible in terms of the Compound, if two conditions are satisfied.

First, cynics and critics must be allowed to continue to reproach man for the bad that he does. Freedom to criticise, freedom of thought and of expression must be allowed as a basic requirement of human life in every society, however unwelcome such expressions may sometimes be.

Second, such cynics and critics must not only have a voice but be listened to, and their warnings and misgivings be acted upon if whenever and wherever found to be valid and action taken when feasible.

As I advised somewhere long ago: scorn not the cynic, for from Heaven he comes and to Heaven he will return. 'Stop being negative!' is one of the worst forms of censorship available in a supposedly civilised and democratic society. The blandishment immediately stifles any further discussion.

History shows, and continues to show, the proclivity of mankind to forget its own lessons, and the more glaringly obvious such lessons are the more they are either ignored or put on the back boiler and effectively forgotten. They didn't listen to Socrates, and this was a gigantic intellectual failing. They didn't listen to Jesus Christ, and this was a gigantic moral failing. They were both executed, for their non-existence was mightily preferred.

But Socrates and Christ are obvious examples of such failings. More worrying are the millions of the nameless who try and fail to get a hearing and are ignored or even worse incarcerated or eliminated in despotic and tyrannical regimes. And let it not be forgotten that even the most revered of democratic societies can also be tyrannical and equally dismissive of the wise and the incisive. Only societies that are fervently and continually on their guard to uphold not only the right to speak but also be heard can ever hope to match material progress, in its multifarious forms, with an equally impressive moral advance. Moral improvement cannot come by itself, nor can it be brought about by the Compound or any of the elements within it.

And so, if an indulgence in simplicity is at least temporarily forgiven, matters stand somewhat thus:

Some place their faith in elements of the Compound exclusive of an external deity – God help them! While those of Faith, who place their trust in a kind of Divine Fixer, have a hell of a wait on their hands!

I recently heard on television a rather rotund and jolly fellow loudly denounce what he called the 'anxiety mongers and negative people' for their dire warnings about the direction Artificial Intelligence might take. All he would say in response to them was, 'Man is great! We can do anything we like! Everything's going to be fine!'

Nobody challenged him. But although I found his 'Man is great!' a most refreshing and welcome change to the even more sinister, though quite meaningless, 'God is Great!' his attitude is as dangerous as stark indifference.

Being a jolly sort of fellow he no doubt lives in a comfortable and successful world inhabited by jokesters and talented pop musicians and enjoys the ability to command the attention of an appreciative, though not particularly deep-thinking, audience. But it is *his* world. It is not *the* world, in which people are ignored or incarcerated or beheaded or blown to smithereens or in so many ways cruelly treated in wars and conflicts. In the world that is not just *his* world, man's inhumanity to man is rife and too often runs riot. In this world that is not his world, man is not so great. Let the jolly fellow step outside his world for a moment and he will most hurriedly step back in. As Primo Levi once famously remarked in *If This Is a Man* (*Se Questo e' Un Uomo'*), man has nothing to boast about ('l'animale umano non ha nulla di cui essere orgolioso').

If there is any hope for moral improvement in the human condition, freedom of thought and of speech must become its universal and unalienable preconditions. But the track record is not inspiring.

As for achieving 'Heaven on Earth', a moral utopia, if it means anything more than the end of war and of man's inhumanity to man, the track record in microcosm is a kind of *reductio ad absurdum*, for it betrays the very principles upon which any real improvement in man's lot should be founded. Those wishing to establish it have succeeded in turning Heaven on Earth into Hell on Earth. Tolstoy's reproach that revolution is one man holding a gun in another man's back applies also to so-called religious 'cults'. The road to Hell does indeed begin with good intentions. The first step is dogma, which cannot be questioned, and it cannot be questioned because it admits of no doubt. Nothing is more dangerous than certainty. Since there is no questioning, those who question are, if fortunate, exiled from the community. Men and women are separated according to a division of labour consequent upon dogma, which almost invariably means that they are considered inferior to men and are without voice, their role confined to the production of babies and the 'care' of the men. Any dissenting voice can expect punishment which, in the absence of contrition, may be inhumanely severe. Such community 'cults' or 'communes' therefore stand their founding principles of equality, freedom and fraternity on their head. Dogma and the questioning it rules out is anathema to improved civilised existence, not its saviour, not its precondition, while sexual abuse and the relegation of women to the sidelines, the bed and the kitchen is simply a rather typical version of man's inhumanity to women.

If this microcosmic track record is anything to go by, a global version would hardly be an improvement upon the mess of the human condition. Phrases like 'Heaven on Earth' must therefore be treated with caution, not to say a bucketful of salt.

But those who wish for something like a future human paradise, a state in which all tears will be washed away, all injustices will be righted, may be compared to the Native American tribes of the MidWest United States in the latter part of the 19th century. They were taught to believe in a time when all their dead would be returned to them, together with the buffalo that the white man had so mindlessly and cruelly shot and skinned. All would be well, and all they had to do was to dance and sing together, wearing shirts of deerskin which would protect them from the bullets of the white man. This was the movement of the so-called Ghost Dance.

Absurd, of course. But it was an expression of deep anguish, a cry of pain and, in modern jargon, 'a coping mechanism'. It was also a false hope *par excellence*. Anguish, pain, frustration and, perhaps above all, disillusionment, lie at the root of Primo Levi's judgement, in *Se Questo e` un Uomo*, that the human animal has nothing to be proud of (l'animale umano non ha nulla di cue essere orgolioso). In vain do we respond by pointing to one technological advance after another or to Michaelangelo's *La Pieta`* or da Vinci's *The Last Supper*. For such works as these cannot meet the moral deficiency of which Levi complains. The work of Mother Teresa would not have saved her from the Nazi persecution had she got in its way. Levi's denunciation of humanity is an expression of pain and acute frustration, as many generalisations are. It is of course a pain that never left him but defined his life indelibly.

One of my teachers, a distinguished philosopher and therefore one whom lesser mortals pass over without a second thought, once gave me an interesting mental picture of a man in bed in pain who tells himself that the pain will be less if only he can turn over onto the other side. The pain will not be less. It might even increase with and after the effort of turning. But it's a speculation that he continues to entertain, false though it is, and, we might add, false though he really knows it to be.

The hope for utopia, for an ultimate fixing and righting of the most unwelcome aspects of the human condition, is also a coping mechanism, a fairy story that helps keep us all going. Compare it also with the conviction that you've had such bad luck that soon your luck is bound to change. This is the Monte Carlo Fallacy, which confuses the chance of throwing a six *after* a certain number of throws with the chance of throwing a six *within* that number. Fallacy or not, it's one that is hard to relinquish, such is the despair and the anguish which inspire its expression.

Even the most irreligious would appeal to God if the circumstances were sufficiently painful, sufficiently pressing. 'God help us!' and 'God help me!' are exclamations that come just as easily from the mouth of the atheist as they well might from Il Papa.

The man in the portrait was certainly not an atheist. No matter. I have no doubt that such cries, inward and outward, came naturally to him as he struggled to come to terms with the fact of war and with the physical pains that beset him during the long, dark hours of night.

Is an end to war and to man's inhumanities to man universally achievable? If this is a real question, the overwhelming evidence suggests that it is impossible. Even the phrase 'overwhelming evidence' fails to hit the mark, for it is in the nature of man that war and inhumanities should continue. Man must cease to be human at all if such a question might be answered in the affirmative, and then of course the question itself would need to be reframed, since man would no longer be its subject. The good news is that it is also in the nature of man to seek the good and condemn the bad. And this means that the fight between good and evil continues, and must continue if evil is not to prevail. Please do not ask which is good and which is evil – if you cannot answer this question in your heart, you will also have difficulty distinguishing black from white. When the fight weakens through the advent of tyrannical power and the fear it engenders, the societies affected are very much the worse for it, but as long as the disease of tyranny and its symptoms remain in the particular and are not spread cancer-like through one society after another, a kind of moral balance of power is the very most that can be expected. The question, 'Which side should the good man be on?' answers itself. The good have no choice at all. And the bad? The bad are as they are, beyond concession, beyond contrition, beyond compromise to a degree determined by how much power they wield over others. In Acton's words, power tends to corrupt and absolute power corrupts absolutely, whether that power is exercised over one individual or over an entire nation or, God help us, over the whole globe. 'Heaven on Earth'? My father spoke of 'life's bitter pathway'. For humans with good intentions it is indeed bitter, but precisely because of the inevitable limits of achievability and the recognition that a 'Heaven on Earth' must contain the seeds of its own corruption and sooner or later become an intolerable nightmare.

What does the portrait say? Does it approve of this line of

reasoning, or does it wince at the number and kind of simplicities? Slow, informed and thoughtful discussion with my father is perhaps what I have missed most by his early demise. Or rather, have I not missed most of all his mere presence, his gentle manner, his reproachful glances? I have missed the power of the good.

21

THOSE WHOM THE GODS LOVE

Those taken prematurely by the gods are beloved not only by the gods but by all those who must live on and suffer their loss. Nor should those loved by the gods feel privileged to be taken so young, for they have missed much. Which raises the question already touched upon elsewhere, namely what exactly have they missed? Perhaps they have missed what Keats called 'the magic hand of chance', for they might have found much comfort in a talent or skill they might have developed had they lived longer. I believe a young friend of Quentin Crisp found something to live for, but too late. A life of depression and dissipation cut his time short just as his artwork was published, and his talent was therefore nipped cruelly in the bud.

If you hitch your wagon to high hopes for the future of mankind, for a permanent end to all war, as though the very concept of war might be relegated to the nursery of mankind, and for a universal end to man's inhumanities, you are likely to find yourself stuck in a mire of disappointment, disillusionment and consequent depression. Some poets have said that rain is the tears of the gods, and rain is only ever temporarily abated.

But hopes may be small as well as big, they may be local as well as universal, they may come in small packages as well as in crates. These are none other than the myriad things that are looked forward to daily. And amongst all these some are bigger than others, more delightful than others, like the hopes we entertain for our children, for their happiness and self-fulfilment. Then there is the mother's hope, all too common, that she will be able to fill the bellies of her children tomorrow, that she will be able to afford the next meal – and if this meagre hope is all too common in the so-called advanced democracies endowed with a concept of social welfare and care, what is to be said about societies in which such a concept is unknown and unwelcome? Hope is therefore relative. Those who are sufficiently affluent entertain no hope that the next meal will be forthcoming, for the next meal is taken very much for granted. But thanks to the inhumanities perpetrated in a multitude of forms, there are too many mothers who hope for the best and expect the worst.

Hopes touching the future of humanity are a luxury for the poor and needy, and discussions and debates concerning it belong to the study and the tutorial. They are rarely found in households scratching for a living. Christ once remarked that we should not worry about tomorrow because the evils of today are sufficient. But those whose bellies cling to their backbones have little choice but to concern themselves with what might or might not come next. Will tomorrow be better than today, or will it be worse? They may entertain thoughts about 'this time next year', but they will hardly go far beyond that. Montaigne said that the sick man has his health up his sleeve, but a man in pain has little choice but to wear his feelings on his sleeve, for pain has an immediacy that can rarely be ignored.

A life cut short is like an unfinished symphony: we may feel invited to guess what the composer intended to come next and how he wished to finish it, assuming that he himself had a clear idea, an assumption that is rather cavalier. Or it is like an unfinished story, and it so often happens that a story develops in the writing and does not, or at least does not entirely, precede it. Writers and composers are entitled to change their minds, even if their intentions seem crystal clear to begin with. Discussions are similar – if they are honest and conducted with more than a smattering of intellectual integrity. Ask someone what he thinks about capital punishment or abortion and his prejudices, if he had any, may be modified or even swept away as he listens to the ebb and flow of discussion and debate. 'I don't know what I think until we have discussed it from all sides, and even then I may not be cocksure' is at least an honest reaction. The process of discursive writing is similar. You begin with an idea which, in the writing, is subject to the death of a thousand qualifications. But quite clearly, too many people end just as they began, as though everything in between had not existed, which is why, although the old and the elderly must in general be respected, wisdom and well-considered judgements do not always lie with them, for age does not necessarily spawn wisdom, and a man may live long but be short on what experience and observation should have taught him. Nor of course does it necessarily lie with the young, still unschooled by 'life's bitter pathway'. Suffering may open the doors to wisdom, but it might also shut them tight.

We do not know and cannot know how my father's story would have unfolded. Perhaps the gods took pity on him for the memories of war he could not escape by any other means than personal extinction. And since long-term memory is said to improve with age, the longer he lived, the sharper they would have become, a profound torment to a sensitive soul. Nor would he have seen the end of war. On the contrary, war after war followed the peace in 1945, including the Cold War and, now, at the time of writing, the threat of global war involving the so-called developed nations which are equipped with nuclear warheads. And all this in societies which have become increasingly violent. The streets are no longer safe, not even in daylight.

He would, however, have enjoyed friendship and the love of loved ones, a favourite meal and a decent cup of tea, a good sleep when tired, and birthdays and Christmases – in other words, all the small things, all the details that enable us to go on in a lighter mood than that dictated by constant reminders of war and inhumanities. Unlike high hopes for the universal moral improvement of mankind, the elimination of war and multifarious forms of inhumanity, hopes for small things often become reasonable expectations, for example the hope for promotion and the reasonable expectation that hard work will be rewarded usually go hand in hand. But let it be remembered that smaller, personal hopes and reasonable expectations cannot compensate for the non-satisfaction of the highest and noblest of hopes, let alone diminish or negate it, but they are a balm which helps us go on despite the worst that humans do. We go on, if not with high hopes for the future of mankind, then at least with a small degree of equanimity and humanity. It would be reasonable to suppose that my father's religion would also have been an important balm, but it is also regrettable that he was not sustained for long on the common man's diet of small hopes and reasonable expectations. What he missed, others who loved him missed also. The gods clearly rule the roost and their decisions overrule our desires, even the unselfish wishes of those who must be left behind to mourn and to grieve. 'As flies to wanton boys are we to the gods, they kill us for their sport,' says Gloucester in *King Lear*, and with ample cause. But this is a one-sided judgement, for the gods show pity also.

What my father's short life demonstrates is the power of the common man, as distinct from the heroes of war and politics or the icons of the arts, to influence the young and become for them a lasting memory and a guiding star. He was a role model without trying to be, a teacher by the power of his personality. He made a lasting and most positive impression, not because he was a father, but because he was the kind of father he was. Everything else about him and what he thought, remains conjecture on my part. The portrait is as fixed as the impression he made. If the portrait is lost or destroyed, the afterimage would remain, the smile indelible, the eyes placid but all-seeing – the whole a message from the past extending into an infinity of futures.

As I recall, my father was a model of patience, placidity and, with the exception of nicotine, extreme moderation. He would not utter an expletive stronger than 'Damn and blast' if he hit his thumb with a hammer, and even this expression of pain would be restrained, muttered and not shouted, which explains why I have not provided a series of exclamation marks. He did his best to teach me restraint, 'When thirsty, sip the water. Never gulp it down.' But I believe his example never really stuck. When my feathers are ruffled I am ready for an emotional blitz even if the seething cauldron remains largely inside my head, thus making me my own worst enemy. 'All or nothing at all' seems to sum me up nicely. I have never been a good student when it comes to self restraint, much to my own annoyance.

My father is an example of a most *uncommon* common man, perhaps the kind that say little but are still capable of setting indelibly good or intriguing examples. His respect for history, for example, was *shown*, not stated, and the showing was not lost on me. Children are not so hot on statements, but they do have eyes to see and minds that work, in the course of time, on what they perceive. My father did not acquire fame, nor did he seek it or lament its deficiency. Setting an effective moral example, being a role model for good, does not require fame as its precondition. On the contrary, fame is often debilitating and self-destructive. Therefore fame is neither a necessary nor a sufficient condition of effective role-modelling. This is of course quite obvious and underlines the importance of parenting. But then, parenting must compete with the influences that technology now presents in the form of social media and so-called 'influencers'. Morally irrelevant and distasteful messages are pedalled to the young and the not-so-young, and parents are obliged to take a back seat due to peer pressure inflated by access to social media and the mindless trumpeting of the merely eccentric and the plainly insane, a fact that does nothing to ameliorate 'life's bitter pathway'.

Children should be returned to their parents, and parents to their children. Is my respect for and gratitude to my father something unique? Certainly not, and we may be thankful for that. But it is also true that children are putty in the hands of those who believe they have something to say on social media websites, and it is also true that many parents have themselves been morally and intellectually degraded by the advent of social media and the consequent widespread dissemination of the banal and the trite. Genuine communication may never have been easy between generations, but now it is harder than ever and fraught with obstacles. In other words, it is harder for parents to be good at parenting. 'Spare the rod and spoil the child' was never intended as a prescription in favour of physical violence, let alone physical abuse. The 'rod' means 'guidance', and the role of parents is that of guides along 'life's bitter pathway'. But so many parents are nowadays incapable of guiding themselves. The blind lead the blind, and they wonder why street gangs, drug abuse and violence could possibly have come about.

It will not have missed the reader that my reflections and remarks are as much about man's predilection towards war, violence and aggression as they are about the particulars remembered touching my father. This is important. For what are we to make of the fact that generation after generation war is remembered, waged, lost or won despite the carnage and inhumanities it engenders? Soldiers may be primary targets, but modern war destroys whole cities whether or not the people who are blown to smithereens support or oppose it. The fallen may be remembered, but that does little or nothing to militate against man's instinct for aggressive survival or violent pursuit of aims. Although he survived the war, my father's life was blighted by it, because war either kills men quickly or it kills them slowly, but no one truly 'survives' war. So-called 'cold wars' are precursors of the real thing.

What does this tell us about humankind? The sheer loss of life and the wholesale destruction of properties and cultural achievements does nothing to even slow the march towards further destruction.

The question of what we are to make of all this is both pressing and perhaps unanswerable, or perhaps it is eminently answerable but the answer is unpalatable. The question, answerable or not, burns into the very fabric of those who have seen war, and those also who have not seen it but who recoil at the very image of it.

22

IN DEFENCE OF REPETITION

The brevity of this last chapter is not evidence of its unimportance. On the contrary, for it is written in the manner of an 'apologia', as distinct from an 'apology', the latter generally connoting regret. It is an explanation or justification of the repeated emphasis placed throughout this book on man's predilection for war, violence, aggression and sundry stark cruelties which come under the heading of 'man's inhumanity to man', notwithstanding the multifarious episodes of kindness, compassion and self-sacrifice that can also be discerned like pin pricks of light on a large black canvas.

My father was daily reminded, as we all are, of the less salubrious aspects of the human animal. It is only necessary to take a casual glance at the daily news to be made aware afresh of man's baser proclivities even if we wish to block them out of our consciousness in favour of our daily routines and, so to speak, the smaller hopes and reasonable expectations which colour our lives and function as welcome diversions from awkward questions about what kind of future our children can expect in a world in which a loving God has been given very much a back seat in this theatre of the absurd.

I have heard a sobering joke to the effect that the difference between humans and animals is that animals would never choose the most stupid amongst them as leaders. Leaders must be strong and authoritative, but their strength and authority must be mediated by an uncommon degree of wisdom and sound judgement. Amongst humans,

147

moral blindness ought to be a summary disqualification for leadership, but the gulf between *what is* and *what ought to be* is nowhere greater in nations which wage aggressive wars with imperialist aims against sovereign states. The degree of wickedness which is blind to the misery and grief that such wars engender amongst soldiers and civilians, and women and children is impossible for the morally enlightened to comprehend. It is this generational, indeed daily, perception of man's inability to be moved by the suffering he causes that tormented my father and torments all like him, added to which is their sheer sense of helplessness in face of what they perceive.

What causes this moral blindness (*cecita` morale*) and how it can be removed is perhaps the most fundamental and most pressing of questions. The answers given may hold little consolation or hope, namely that we are stuck with what we have, that we can merely seek to manage the phenomenon, like a medical condition that cannot be cured but only managed. But management may fail, partly because the 'patients' are ignorant of the fact that they have a condition that should be treated. A patient who wrongly believes he has no tumour will not be ready to suffer surgery to extract it.

Whatever the analysis, whatever theories are put forward touching these dreadful aspects of the everlasting human condition, the fact is that, in modern parlance, *it is what it is*. That said, humanity can only hope that there will always be those who are ready to question and reprove, criticise and rebuke, protest and rebuff those who, by some deplorable twist of fate, become the tyrannical leaders of the common man, who asks for nothing more than to live with dignity and at peace with his neighbours. Regrettably, the 'common man' so often fails to recognise the evil that his leaders do, for the common man is also human and therefore shares with his leaders the failings of his nature.

Meanwhile, I grow old and the portrait grows younger in comparison, a glowing example, in a plain wooden frame, of hope and perhaps no small degree of expectation, and the old man who looks upon it frowns at a world which is in real and ever present danger of repeating all the wars and all the repression and all the inhumanities that ever were. The gap between the portrait and he who sees it grows larger, as does that between the lessons that should have been learned and those who should know better.

Through my father, I continue to converse with myself in the darkness of our times. Human life also goes on. Those who dare to speak of the 'moral progress' of humankind as though the phrase made perfect and unequivocal sense should remember that simple linear progression does not exist in the mathematics of human affairs and that it is infinitely easier to move backwards than it is to move forwards. Every creature of a profoundly reflective disposition, afflicted with hypersensitivity, requires a companion. Mine has been my father *in absentia*. But who will be the companions of future generations on 'life's bitter pathway'? Who will the young turn to when the gates of Hell are flung wide on their hinges? Or will the very concept of role model no longer be extant?

23

BEING OLDER THAN MY FATHER

I am now much older than the young man in the portrait, and might even qualify as his grandfather. I am also much older than the man I remember who later died in his late 40s, and might qualify as his father. There is something discomforting about this, perhaps because it is an odd but inescapable reminder that life's candle burns down faster and lower for some than for others, and that mine is now on its last few laps. Some candles are shorter than others, and some might seem unjustly long. I feel undeserving of longevity, having little to contribute to any recognised human activity such as politics, sport, medicine, education or the arts. The world could well do without me, and when my candle is finally spent it will be ignorant of the fact that I ever drew breath. It is a worrying if not tragic reflection that so many humans die without first having lived, and it is also disconcerting that so many die without ever leaving so much as a footprint on the sands of time.

I have sometimes tried to imagine my father as an old man, old enough even not to have such things as artificial intelligence or drone attacks explained to him. As it is, I play the role of the old man endeavouring to explain to the young man in the portrait what such things are, and were that young man a sentient being and not simply a representation he would perhaps call to mind Wells's *The War of the Worlds* or Wyndham's *The Day of the Triffids*, and his astonishment would be matched by his dismay that human beings have regressed so far that they beat up cities and decimate populations while still considering themselves sane and reasonable. As for his later self who joined the Royal Artillery, was defeated at Dunkirk and then died prematurely in peacetime of a 'coronary thrombosis', he too would be bitterly disappointed that mankind that once again failed to learn lessons and was now using instruments of death that far outranked the field guns that he helped maintain and to fire.

I use the word 'prematurely' with some caveats. Montaigne remarks somewhere that dying of old age is uncommon and that most die much sooner or disease and other accidents of fate. But he was writing in the mid-to-late 16th century when reaching old age was far less a possibility than it is now. Medical science was still in one of its many infancies, and expectations of longevity were at a low. Now, as politicians are keen to remind us, we are living with an aging population, which these worthies take as an excuse to curtail benefits and trim back pensions, as though the aged were accustomed to living it up in their final decades and had no earthly right to do so. Since life expectation is that much higher than it was in Montaigne's day, it is reasonable to say that my father died 'prematurely' since, other things being equal, he might have been expected to live into his 70s, 80s, or even 90s. Of course, other things were not equal, nor are they for many if not most of us. Indeed, although more people live into old age now, defined as their 70s and 80s, relatively few live longer, and if statistics were compiled it might still be true that most people die before what we can reasonably call 'old age'. The human proclivity for war and inhumanity seem to ensure that many people will not see out their teens, while many will feel the hand of death in their very cradles.

No doubt, being a reflective man, my father thought of old age and how he might cope with it, little expecting that he would never reach it. As the years tick by, as the candle burns lower and lower still, such thoughts are natural, as are thoughts of death and how and where and when you are going to have to face it. As to the nature of death, I believe it was Wittgenstein who remarked that death is not a move *within* a game but the end of the game. It is dying, not death, that is experienced, for we cannot experience our own death, although of course we experience the death of others. As to the latter, my mother would remark, 'Well, it's a nine-day wonder. We're soon forgotten.'

Perhaps the death of someone we do not know, or hardly know, is, as my mother said, simply a nine-day wonder. But it is patently and painfully obvious that the death of a loved one is far from being a nine-day wonder, but may be instead an indelible and profoundly impressionable event in the lives of those who experience the death of a loved one or someone they deeply respected or admired. We cannot experience our own death, but the experience of that of others may have an inspiring or a devastating effect on those who are left behind to mourn and to remember, as the effects of the portrait of my young father and memories of his later self have, I hope, clearly testified.

What we can experience is also what we can imagine, and what we can imagine may be fearful. My own death is a state of non-being, which cannot be experienced and so cannot be imagined, and therefore cannot be feared. I can imagine an empty room with my corpse lying there, but I cannot imagine my state of non-being. I can imagine the process of dying, for I know what sleep and pain are, I know what illness is, and I have seen others close to death. I can also certainly imagine the predicament of those affected by my death, because I know what loss and grief are. What may certainly be feared is the effect of my death on others, for I would leave them to face the world alone. Not that my living would guarantee that I could solve the problems they encounter in the course of their lives. But the raw irony is that my demise would mean leaving my loved ones to fend for themselves in a world I have spent so long reproaching and holding in contempt. And this thought is most unsavoury. In this sense, 'fear of one's own death' means fearing the repercussions for loved ones. I can imagine being tortured or incarcerated or bound hand and foot, and therefore I can fear them. I cannot fear my state of non-being, because I cannot know what it is I am supposed to imagine, but I can clearly imagine its consequences for some others.

Are these reflections correct, or are they fallacious? I look elsewhere for some validation, for some confirmation that I am on the right track or else have taken a number of wrong turnings. Can you imagine nothingness? An empty sky will not do. Can you imagine your own nothingness? If I read a history book, I am reading about events I did not witness – perhaps this is as close as we can get to imagining our own nothingness – but these are events in the *past*, not in the present. The search for validation must continue.

A civilisation may be morally measured by how far it respects the dead, and therefore the living, for the dead were once living and their virtues and vices, their wisdom and ignorance can hardly be worse than that of those who outlive them. Those who die remain loved by those who survive them if the ties were close and perhaps intimate. The death of strangers is to be lamented, and only a release from unbearable pain and incurable terminal disease can get anywhere near to validating it. Respect for the dead, for all those who have gone before, is the flip side of respect for the living. If a society shows little respect for those who live, what then can be expected of it for those whose lives have been extinguished? A society which has become increasingly violent is a society which is increasingly disrespectful of human life, and therefore those who are close to death, like those who have already expired, can expect little respect or affection lest it come from those who love them deeply.

I have noted that afternoon television, watched mainly by retirees and the elderly, punctuates its entertainment with commercials for funerals and cremation, with companies vying with one another and promising the cheapest, quickest and most effective road to complete annihilation. Whether we come from dust is uncertain, but such companies are determined that to dust we shall return. Apart from the insensitivity that such a repetition of commercials unquestionably entails, the general effect is to render death simply one event amongst others, as though soap power or a holiday in Marbella were on offer, thus degrading the profundity of death. But this is to be expected when, at the time of writing, respect for life is at a very low ebb and when women and girls can hardly walk the streets of London without fear of attack or some form of abuse. As for the concept 'the sanctity of human life', the phrase is now as hollow as an old oak.

There are other, far more discreet, means of informing people of their funerary options, but the advertising industry, despite regulatory measures, is not universally praised for its moral sagacity or its meticulous attention to the deeper sensibilities of the various publics it targets.

(I confess that I have never been able to accept the fact of death, and whatever this admission might mean, it cannot be rebutted by the provision of a physiological explanation or a submission to logic.)

As I stare at the portrait of my young and handsome father, I spot my own ghostly image in the glass and wonder who it can possibly be. Who owns this tired, lined and bespectacled face? When young I might have checked myself in the mirror to assure myself that I was a fairly reasonable catch for any young maiden whose expectations did not exceed my own. But now, the mirror is a deceiving elf. I have heard it said that it is beneficial, to own more than one mirror, placing each in a different room, because, depending on certain factors, including light and shade and the time of day, your reflection looks younger or older or more or less fairer depending on the mirror you look into, so that, disappointed with one mirror, you might find improvement in another.

I am not in favour of mirror hopping. Such vanities left port long ago. But I often glance unbelieving at my own image, finding it hard to recognise with any immediacy. There seems nothing but contrast between that image and that of my youthful father. The portrait represents hope for the future; my own, regrets for the past and forebodings of what is to come. I believe that my father met his end unexpectedly, with no time to reflect upon how it might be prepared for. I, on the other hand, have all the time in the world and can only hope that I meet death calmly and with a gentle resignation. Thomas's 'Do not go gentle into that good night, Old age should burn and rave at close of day, Rage, rage against the dying of the light' does little for me. My rage, my burning and raving began long ago when I could see what a hopeless mess humans have made and are making and will make of anything and everything that might be called 'beautiful'. For I have seen that when men speak of peace they mean war, hate when they speak of love, and ugliness when they speak of beauty. I have heard some who wax lyrical about mass destruction and the fire of destruction, calling such horrors 'beautiful'. Even some who were the target of the bomb at Hiroshima called the cloud 'beautiful' while others were skinned alive under it. In such a topsy-turvy world of bitter consequences, there is much scope for rage, a rage that should not wait for the close of day.

Sitting with my father now, were it possible, would be a sad thing, as though we sat in the ruins of a house, barely a wall still standing, and were trying to see some light on a dark horizon. I prefer therefore to think that he had his time as I have mine, that he made the best of his as I must endeavour to make the best of mine. There is no idle sentimentality here, just life as we must each live it each according to his understanding, warts and all, and this in the darkness of a time that the most uncommon of common men have little chance of alleviating.

Perhaps it is fitting to spare a thought for those who may think that my knowledge of my father is too scant to form a clear idea of the man and that my appraisal of him as 'a most uncommon common man' is born more of natural sentiment than of hard evidence. It is true of course that it is hardly possible to delineate a person in a few sentences or even in a book, and I would not dare claim to do so. How much can one person know of another? It has been rightly said that no man is an island unto himself. Yet each man is like an island in that you may sail around him many times and for many years, perhaps even over a lifetime, and never quite manage to beach your craft and reach dry land, let alone the interior. The inner man must remain in shadow and the telescope through which we perceive him is a glass through which we see darkly. Married couples and partners know each other intimately, but never completely. Intimacy is not synonymous with completeness, and yet the one is generally confused with the other.

If the inner man must remain in shadow, there are sparks of light which illuminate and inform and which go beyond mere sentiment or imagined reciprocity of feeling between father and son. Solzhenitsyn somewhere remarks that there is a feeling that something is true, a feeling that someone or something is sincere or genuine, a feeling which distinguishes between true and false, between truth and fake. If all we are left with is such a feeling we should cling to it with all our might.

In the portrait I see a man of integrity and of depth, and the illuminating sparks of evidence that I have described throughout this book are sufficient at least to intimate the inner man even though that inner man must remain unreachable in its entirety, as though lying on the bottom of an inaccessible well. An insoluble mystery now in death, as we must all become, but insoluble anyway, for I cannot see through his eyes any more than I can yours, or you mine.

But it has been said that the health of a tree is known by its fruit. Then similarly, the worth of a man, his inner self, is known, as far as it can be known, by the lessons he teaches and the values he embodies thereby. My father taught me, and forever reminds me, that 'life's bitter pathway' is a road best taken in the company of friends and kindred spirits. Not alone, unless Fate so decrees it, for then we are left to rely on our comparatively slender resources and the tender gaze of a loving God. The lesson of loving and selfless companionship shines through the eyes of the man in the portrait and was never lost even when those same eyes grew old and tired from doleful memories and burgeoning disease. 'Look after them' were his last words to those assembled on his demise, where 'them' was my mother and me. These are words we should all use for one another, if only the world of men would permit it. Instead, mankind mindlessly walks 'life's bitter pathway' as though there is nothing for it but to suffer alone, not the slings and arrows of outrageous fortune, but the weapons of war and of so-called peace that men themselves fashion to outdo and suppress one another, as though they did not share a common fate but could outrank one another even in a 'life hereafter'.

I have used the word 'Fate' more often than I should wish, and I have referred to what Fate might 'decree'. It is true that we must often submit to the force of circumstance, but the role of so-called Fate in the lives of humans is also so often and so mindlessly overplayed. Should we call 'inevitable' the destruction of cities, the laying waste of countries, the genocide of peoples and the extinction of whole cultures? What seems inescapable is that the power welded by man is not that of love but of submission, with consequences that man is apt to attribute to something called Fate. Here, I never tire of quoting Homer, who hit the mark long, long ago:

Perverse mankind! whose wills, created free,

Charge all their woes on absolute decree;

All to the dooming gods their guilt translate,

And follies are miscalled the crimes of fate.

(*The Odyssey*, Bk 1, lines 40–44)

And one of the most grotesque and demonstrably irrepressible of man's follies is the driving of the weak into blind and morally indefensible forms of submission. Men are forever in search of ways in which they can call themselves better than their fellows, which is why they seek hegemony over countries and peoples. The 'argument of force' must of course be resisted, first by the 'force of argument' and then, when that fails, as it almost invariably does, aggression is met with counter-aggression, and so conflict ensues with all its miseries. Men should first seek to better themselves before they attempt to instruct others, and self-betterment knows no end. And let a man submit to love before he submits to anything else.

This is a corollary of the lesson I learned from my father. People should live side by side, not one on top of the other. In the words of the song, a man should walk through the dark with his head held high – but not forgetting to place his hand in that of another! 'Life's bitter pathway' is best walked together.

*****